BEGINNING GAMES

A Tisket A Tasket

Matching Games for Colors, Shapes & Patterns

by Marilynn G. Barr

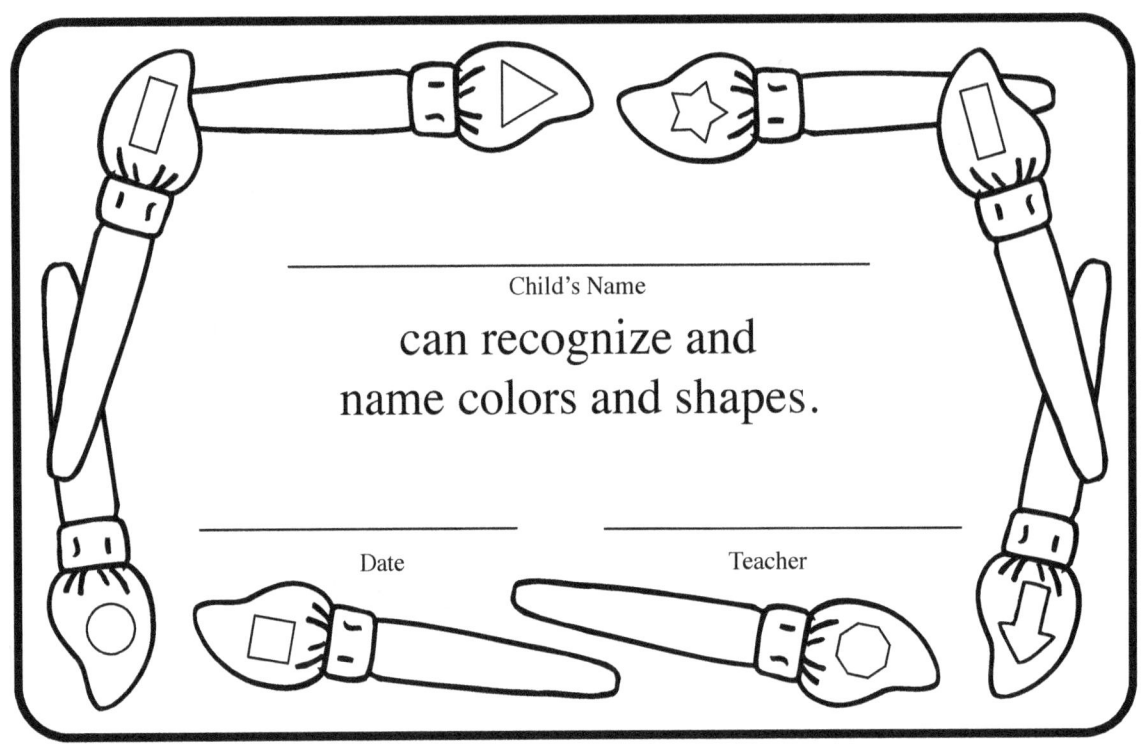

_____
Child's Name

can recognize and name colors and shapes.

_____ _____
Date Teacher

LAB20139
Beginning Games
A TISKET A TASKET
by Marilynn G. Barr

Published by: Little Acorn Books™
Originally published by: Monday Morning Books, Inc.

Entire contents copyright © 2013 Little Acorn Books™

Little Acorn Books
PO Box 8787
Greensboro, NC 27419-0787

Promoting Early Skills for a Lifetime™

Little Acorn Books™
is an imprint of Little Acorn Associates, Inc.

http://www.littleacornbooks.com

Permission is hereby granted to reproduce student materials in this book for non-commercial individual or classroom use. *School-wide or system-wide use is expressly prohibited.

ISBN 978-1-937257-43-9

Printed in the United States of America

A Tisket A Tasket

Contents

Introduction 4	Cover 43
Heart to Heart 5	Game Board 44
Game Board 6	Game Cards 46
Game Cards 8	Door Patterns and Key Game Cards ... 47
Cover 10	Turnip Patch Match 48
Buttons and Bows 11	Cover 49
Game Board 12	Game Board 50
Game Cards 14	Game Cards 52
Cover 16	Duck, Duck, Goose 54
A Tisket a Tasket 17	Cover 55
Game Board 18	Game Board 56
Game Cards 20	Game Cards 58
Cover 22	Hat Stackers 60
Bounce 23	Game Board 61
Game Board 24	Game Cards 63
Bouncing Bear Patterns 25	
Game Cards 29	
Ships Ahoy! 30	
Game Board 31	
Ship Patterns 32	
Game Cards 35	
Paint a Palette 38	
Game Board 39	
Game Cards 41	
Knock Knock 42	

A Tisket A Tasket

Introduction

Children enjoy plenty of color, shape, and pattern matching practice with the ready-to-use beginning games featured in *A Tisket A Tasket*. Players learn to follow directions, practice fair-play, and develop readiness, fine-motor, and memory skills. Game formats include trail games, match boards, clothespin games, and stackers. Every game includes a game board and programmed playing pieces.

Children match shapes and patterns on Heart to Heart, Buttons and Bows, and A Tisket a Tasket trail games. Bounce, Ships Ahoy!, and Paint a Palette clothespin games offer shape, pattern, and color skills practice as well as fine motor skills development. Children clip clothespin game cards to matching balls, ships, and paint spots. Knock Knock, Turnip Patch, and Duck, Duck, Goose match board games encourage visual discrimination. Players match key, turnip, duck, and goose cutout game cards to the correct spaces on each game board. Hat Stackers offers self-checking multi-dimensional skills practice as children identify and stack matching hat game cards.

A Tisket A Tasket Tic-Tac-Toe For Two Players

Children develop visualization and strategy skills as they play tic-tac-toe. Reproduce, color, laminate, and cut apart the game board and cards. Each player chooses the carrot or basket cards. In turn, each player places a card on one of the tic-tac-toe spaces. The first player with three carrots or baskets in a row, vertically, horizontally, or diagonally, wins.

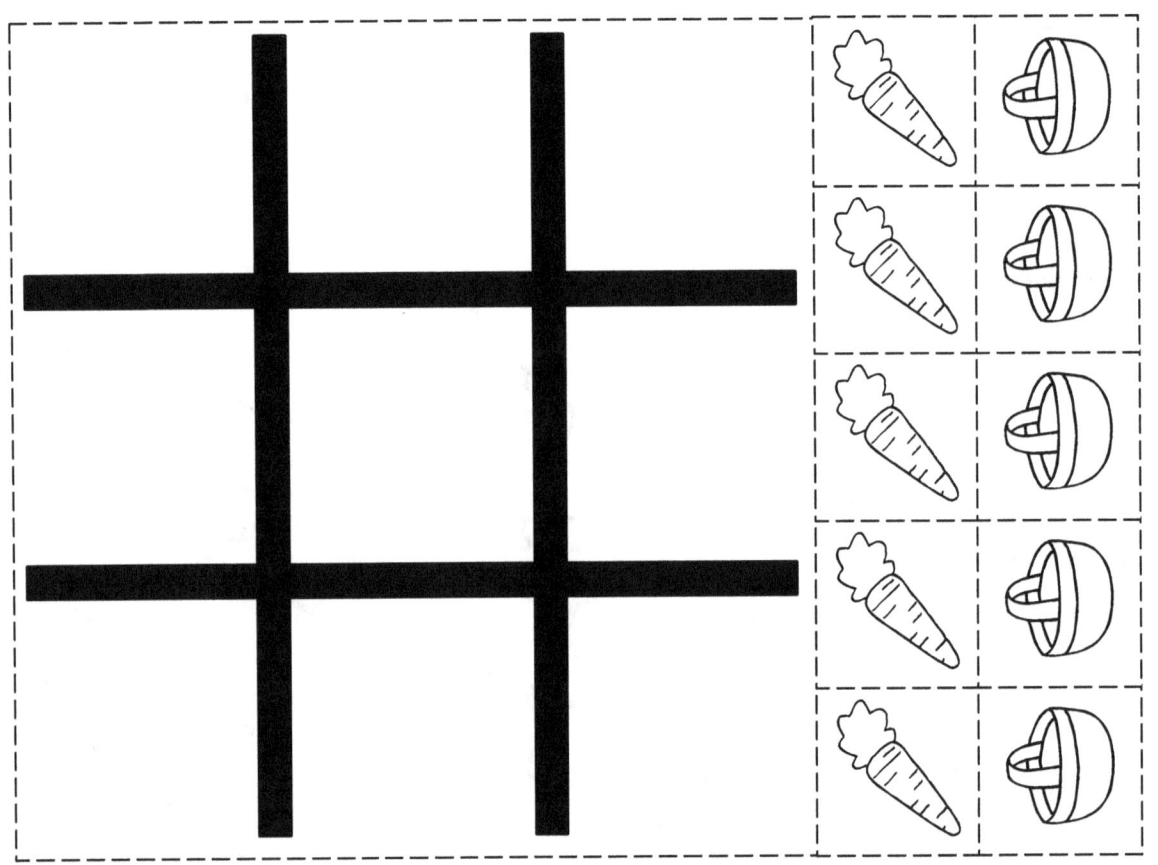

Heart to Heart
A Trail Game
For Two to Four Players

Pawns

Materials
crayons, markers, scissors, glue, file folder, envelope, tape

Assembly
Game Board: Reproduce, color, and cut out the cover and game board patterns. Matching in the center, glue the game board patterns to the inside of a folder. Glue the cover to the front of the folder, then laminate. Tape an envelope to the back of the game board folder to store pawns and game cards.

Pawns: Reproduce, color, laminate, and cut out a set of pawns. Store the pawns in the envelope on the back of the folder.

Game Cards: Reproduce, color, laminate, then cut apart the heart game cards. Option: Reproduce, color, and glue each page of cards to the back of a sheet of gift wrap, then laminate, and cut apart the cards. Store the game cards in the envelope on the back of the game board folder.

How to Play
Set up a game board and cards on a table. Each player chooses a pawn. Then one player shuffles and places the deck of cards, face down, on the table. Each player, in turn, draws a card and moves his or her pawn to the next matching space on the game board. Drawn cards are placed, face down, in a discard pile. Play continues until each player reaches The End. When all the cards have been drawn, reshuffle the discard pile and continue playing.

Heart to Heart Game Board

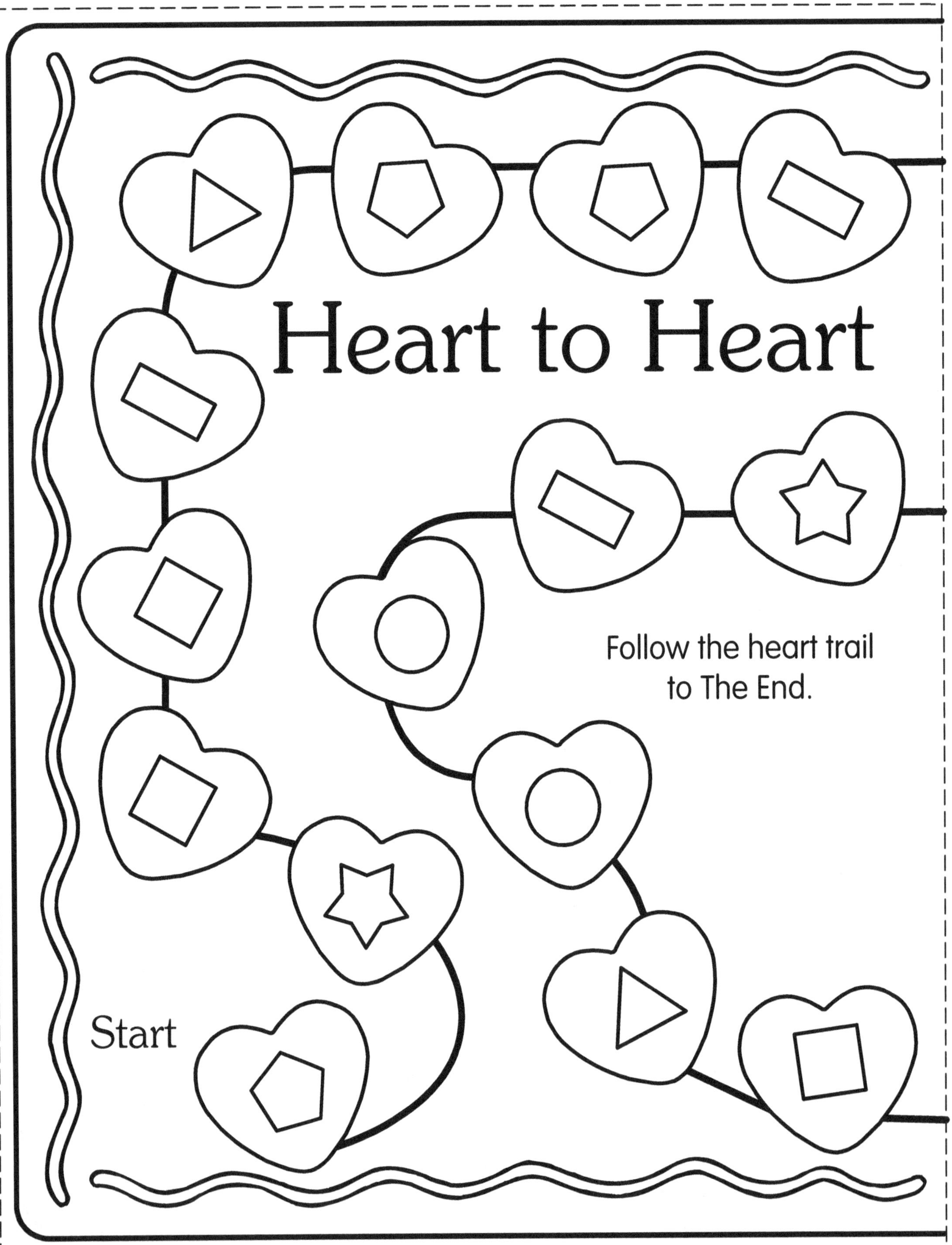

Heart to Heart

Follow the heart trail to The End.

Start

Heart to Heart Game Board

Heart Game Cards

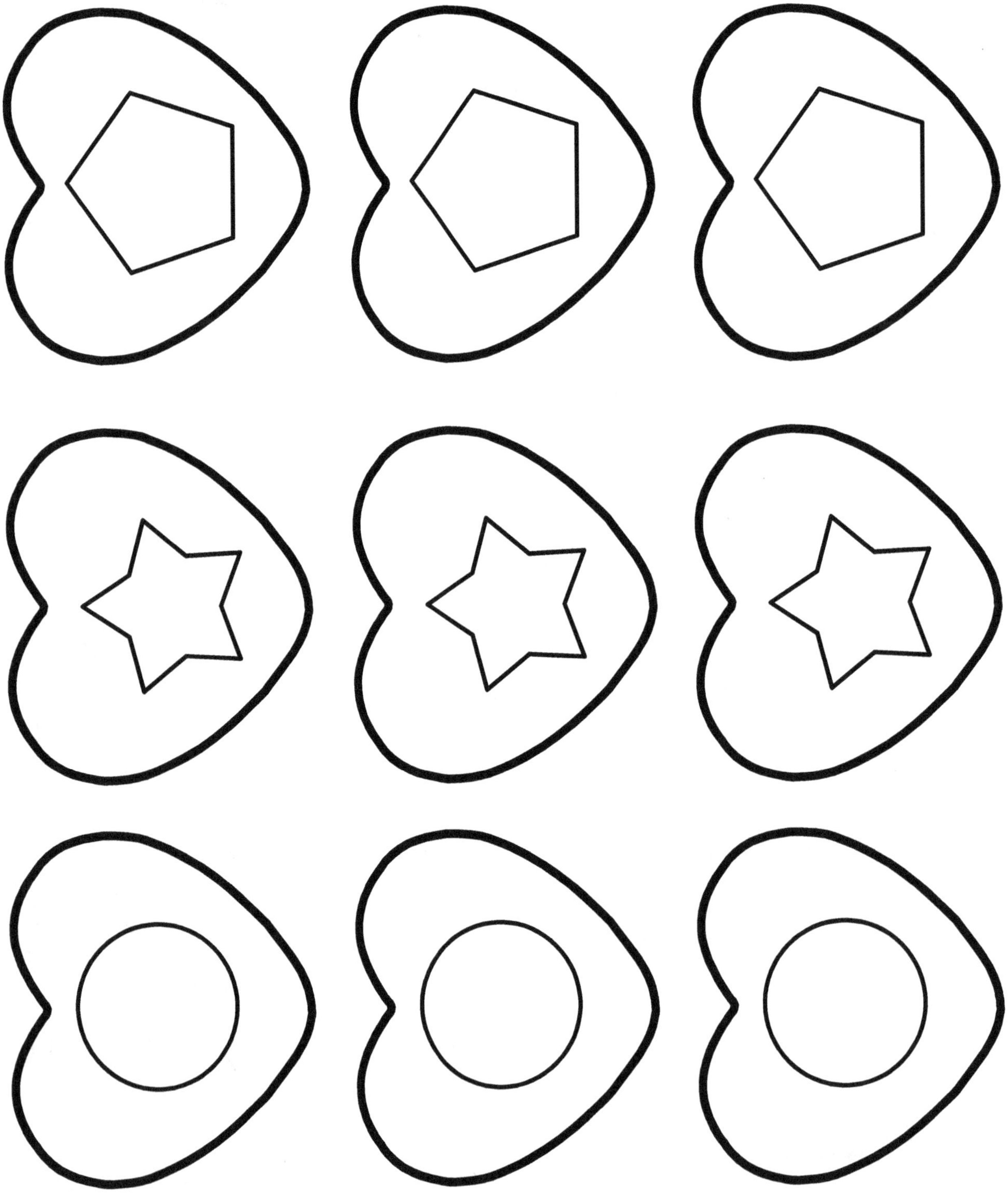

Reproduce, color, and cut out one set of game cards for a game of Heart to Heart.
Creative Option: Reproduce, color, and cut out the heart cards. Punch a hole on each side of each heart cutout. Measure, cut, and lace a necklace length of yarn through the holes in each heart to form a necklace.

LAB20139 • A TISKET A TASKET • 978-1-937257-43-9 • © 2013 Little Acorn Books™

Heart Game Cards

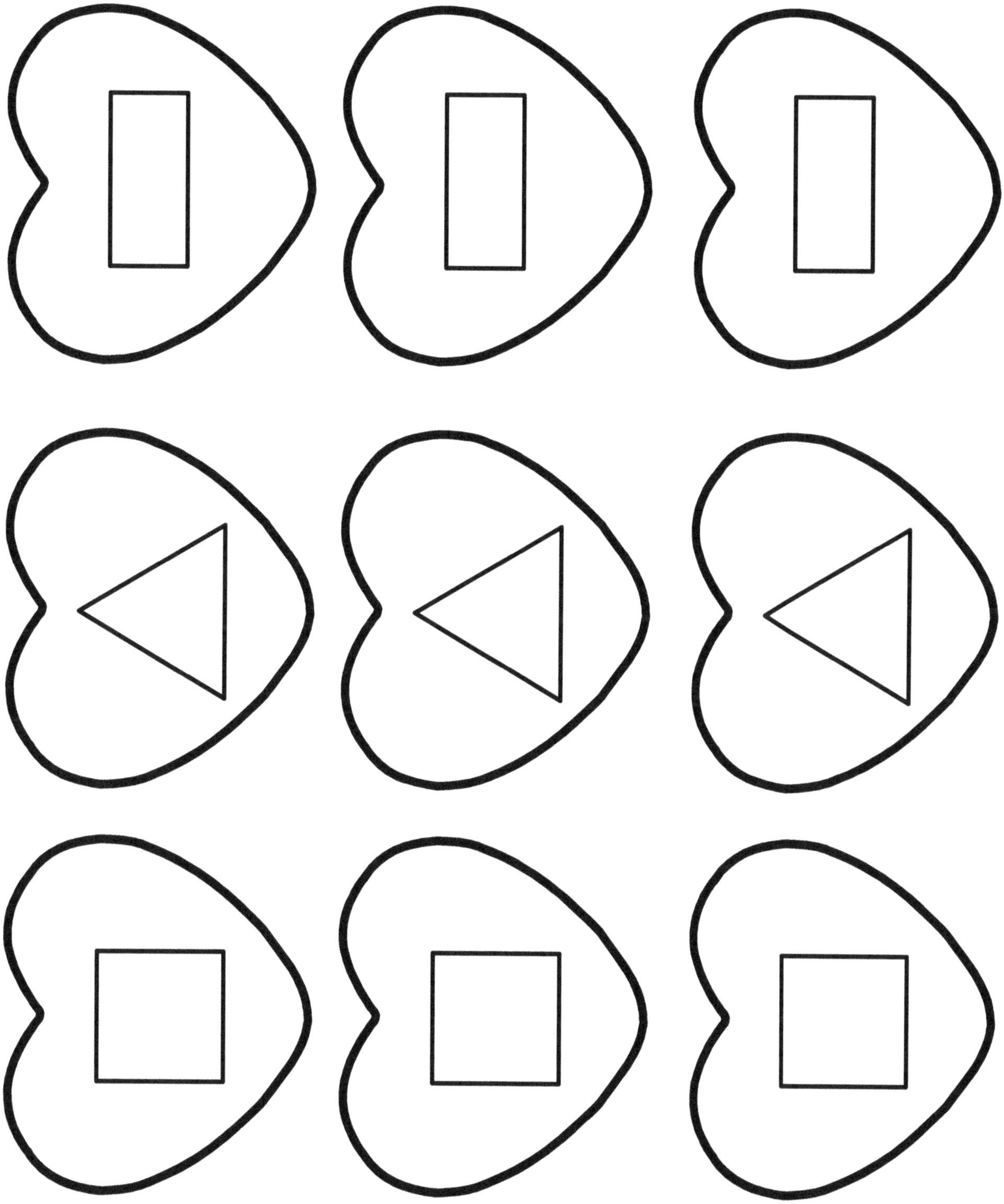

Reproduce, color, and cut out one set of game cards for a game of Heart to Heart.
Creative Option: Reproduce, color, and cut out two sets of heart cards to make a
deck of Concentration cards. Color pairs to match.

Heart to Heart Cover

Buttons and Bows
A Trail Game
For Two to Four Players

Materials
crayons, markers, scissors, glue, file folder, envelope, tape

Assembly
Game Board: Reproduce, color, and cut out the cover and game board patterns. Matching in the center, glue the game board patterns to the inside of a folder. Glue the cover to the front of the folder, then laminate. Tape an envelope to the back of the game board folder to store pawns and game cards.

Pawns: Reproduce, color, laminate, and cut out a set of pawns. Store the pawns in the envelope on the back of the folder.

Game Cards: Reproduce, color, laminate, then cut apart the button and bow game cards for a shapes matching activity. Option: Reproduce, color, and glue each page of game cards to the back of a sheet of gift wrap, then laminate, and cut apart the cards. Store the game cards in the envelope on the back of the game board folder.

How to Play
Set up the game board and cards on a table. Each player chooses a pawn. One player shuffles and places the deck of cards, face down, on the table. Each player, in turn, draws a card and moves his or her pawn to the next matching space on the game board. Drawn cards are placed, face down, in a discard pile. Play continues until each player reaches the Button Box at The End. When all the cards have been drawn, reshuffle the discard pile and continue playing.

Pawns

Buttons and Bows Game Board

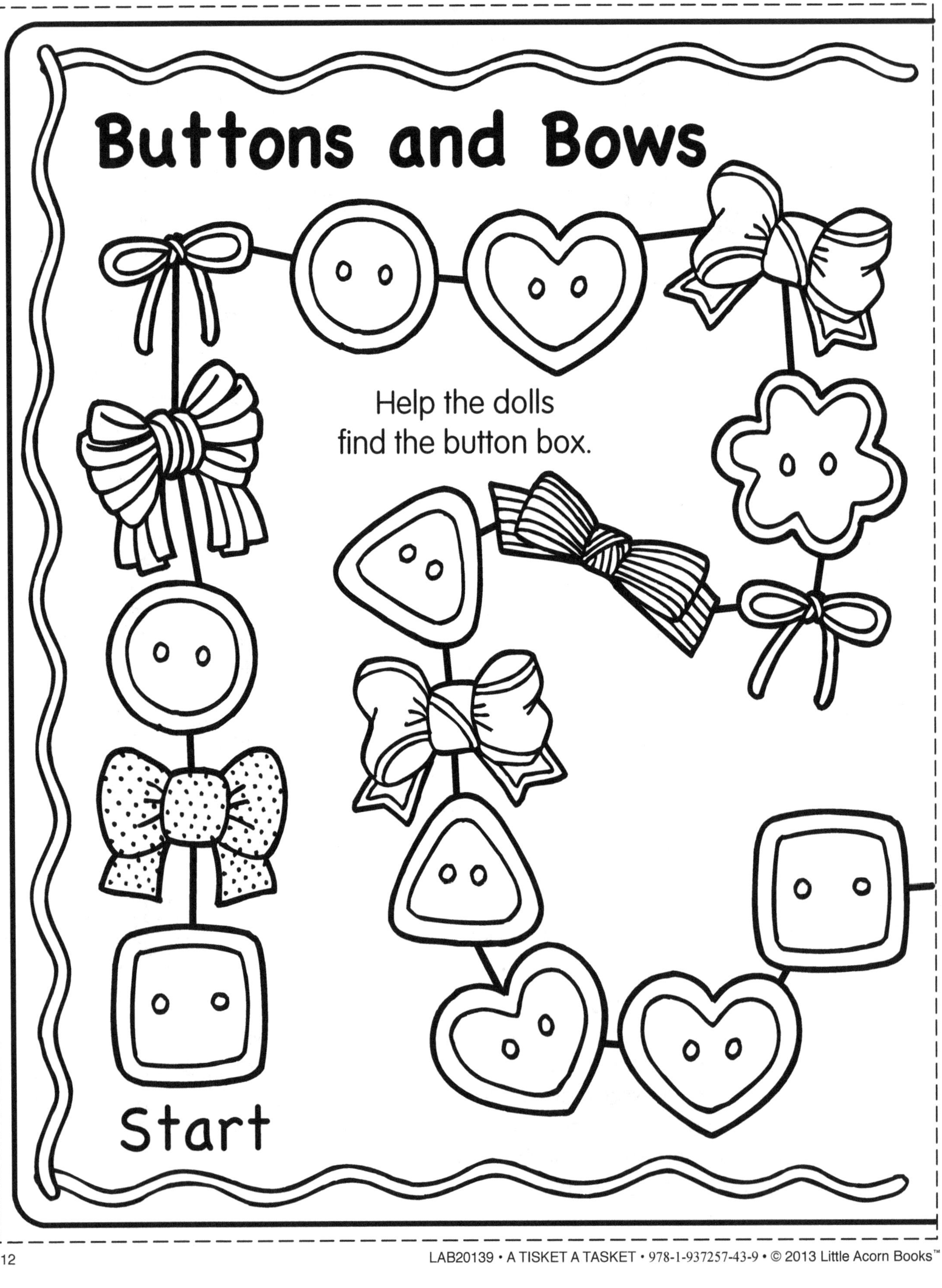

Buttons and Bows

Help the dolls find the button box.

Start

Buttons and Bows Game Board

Button and Bow Game Cards

Option: Reproduce red, blue, yellow, green, purple, and orange game cards for a color matching activity. Color the button spaces on the game board to match.

Example: Color a round blue button space on the game board to match a round blue button card.

Creative Option: Reproduce, color, cut out, and glue the buttons to a folded sheet of construction paper to make a greeting card. Write a message inside the card.

Button and Bow Game Cards

Option: Reproduce red, blue, yellow, green, purple, and orange game cards for a color matching activity. Color the bow spaces on the game board to match.

Example: Color a polka dot bow space yellow on the game board to match a yellow polka dot bow card.

Creative Option: Provide each child with a bow card, a colored construction paper square or rectangle, and a length of yarn to make gift box displays. Help each child cut out and glue a yarn ribbon on his or her shape as shown. Then have children color, cut out, and glue their bows on their shape gift boxes.

Buttons and Bows Cover

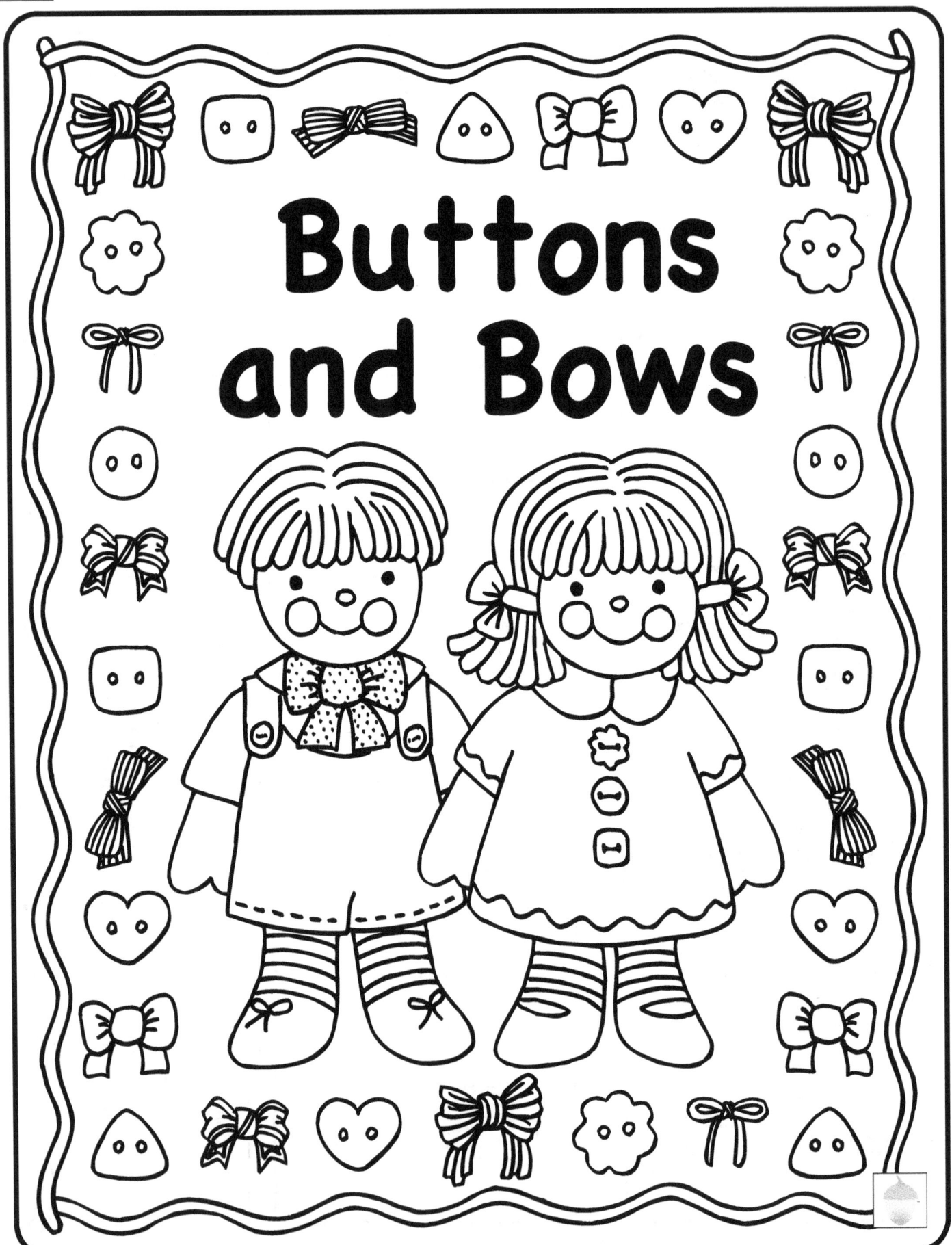

A Tisket a Tasket
A Trail Game
For Two to Four Players

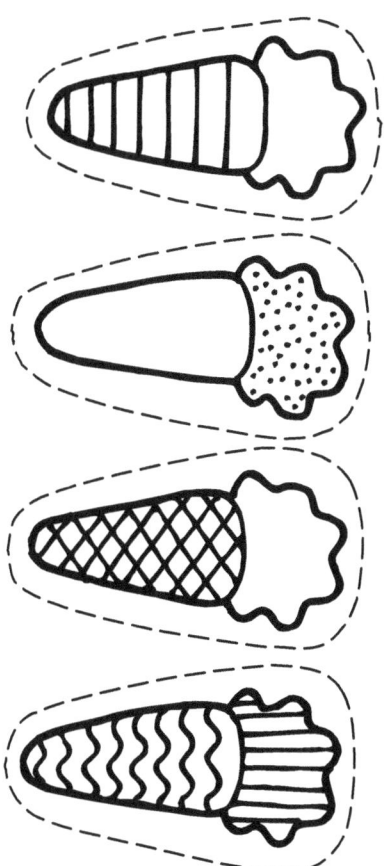

Pawns

Materials
crayons, markers, scissors, glue, file folder, envelope, tape

Assembly
Game Board: Reproduce, color, and cut out the cover and game board patterns. Matching in the center, glue the game board patterns to the inside of a folder. Glue the cover to the front of the folder, then laminate. Tape an envelope to the back of the game board folder to store pawns and game cards.

Pawns: Reproduce, color, laminate, and cut out a set of pawns. Store the pawns in the envelope on the back of the folder.

Game Cards: Reproduce, color, laminate, then cut apart two sets of game cards. Option: Reproduce, color, and glue each page of game cards to the back of a sheet of gift wrap, then laminate and cut apart the cards. Store the game cards in the envelope on the back of the game board folder.

How to Play
Set up the game board and cards on a table. Each player chooses a pawn. One player shuffles and places the deck of cards, face down, on the table. Each player, in turn, draws a card and moves his or her pawn to the next matching space on the game board. Drawn cards are placed, face down, in a discard pile. Play continues until each player reaches the rabbit's basket at The End. When all the cards have been drawn, reshuffle the discard pile and continue playing.

A Tisket a Tasket Game Board

A Tisket a Tasket Game Board

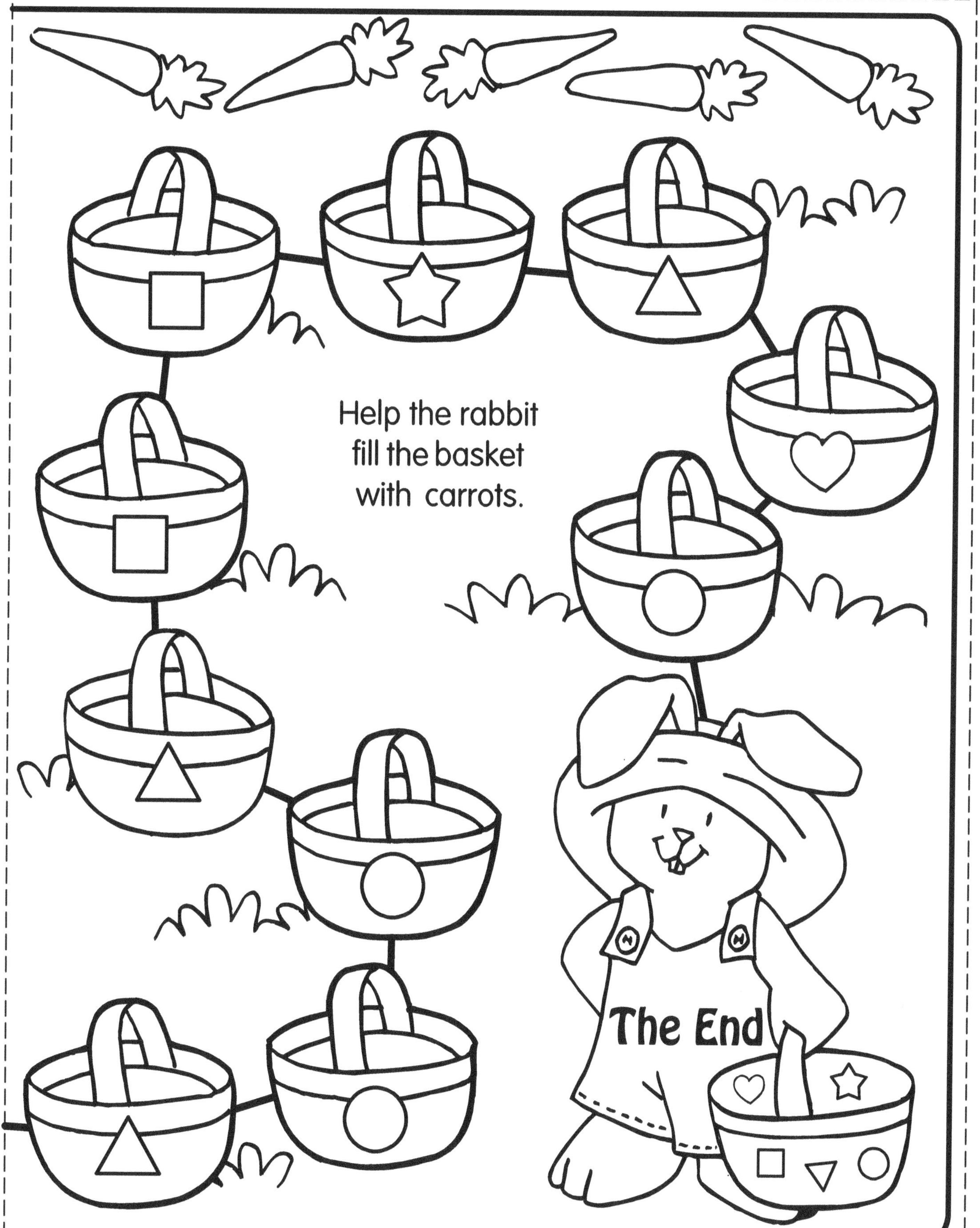
Help the rabbit
fill the basket
with carrots.
The End

Shape Basket Game Cards

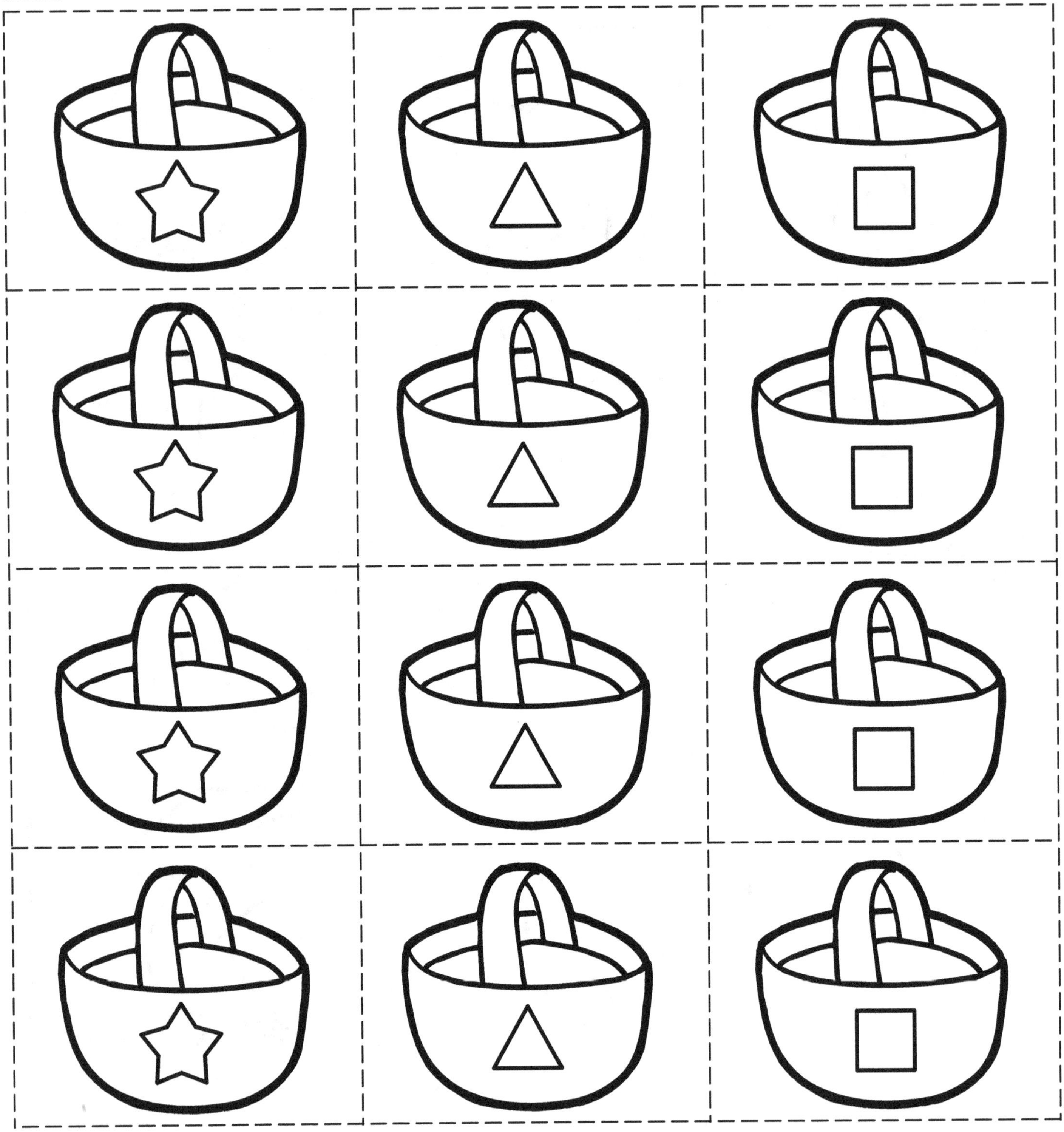

Reproduce, color, and cut out two sets of game cards for a game of A Tisket a Tasket.

Option: Reproduce red, blue, yellow, green, purple, and orange game cards for a color matching activity. Color the basket spaces on the game board to match.

Example: Color a circle basket on the game board blue to match a blue circle basket game card.

Shape Basket Game Cards

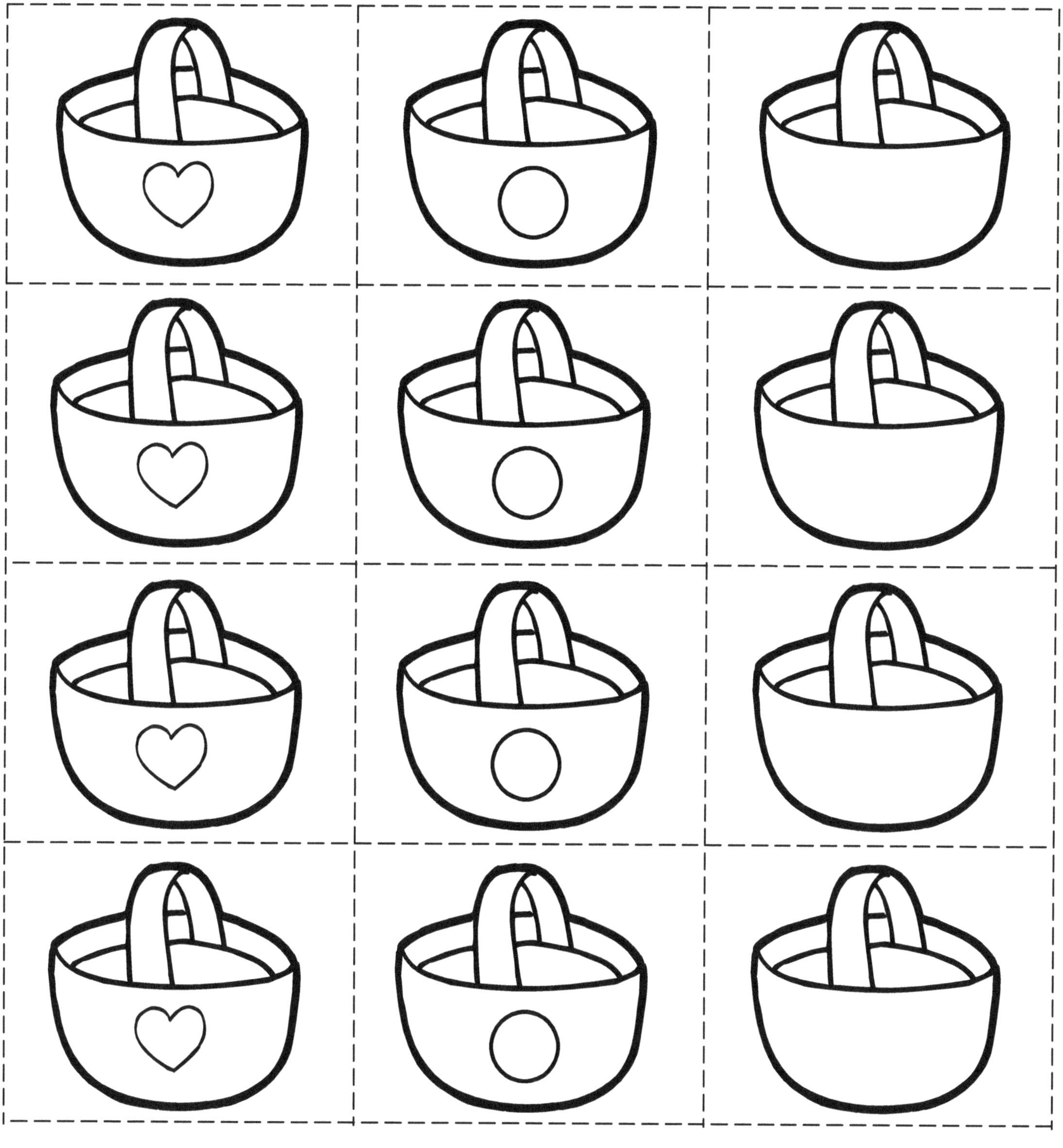

Reproduce, color, and cut out two sets of game cards for a game of A Tisket a Tasket.

Creative Option: Reproduce, color, and cut out red, blue, yellow, green, orange, and purple baskets. Attach a magnetic square to the back of each basket. Use a permanent marker to decorate the border around a cookie sheet to use as a playing surface. Children can match baskets by shape or color.

A Tisket a Tasket Cover

A Tisket A Tasket

Bounce
A Clothespin Game
For Two Players

Materials
crayons, markers, scissors, glue, file folders, clothespins, large envelope

Assembly
Game Board: Reproduce, color, and cut out four game board patterns. Matching along the straight edges, glue the game board patterns on a poster board circle to form a round game board. Glue the title in the center of the game board. Then reproduce, color, cut out, and glue eight bouncing bear patterns on the assembled game board. Note: Make multiple boards to practice all featured shapes.

Clothespin Game Cards: Reproduce, color, and cut out a set of ball game cards. Glue a clothespin to the back of each game card. Decorate a large envelope with colored construction paper circles. Store the clothespin game cards in the envelope. (Include non-matching game cards for advanced players, or all matches for early learners.)

How to Play
Set up the game board on a table. Place the clothespin game cards, face down, on the table. Each player, in turn, draws a clothespin. If there is a match, the player identifies the match, and clips the clothespin to the correct space. If there is no match, the player places the clothespin back on the table, face down. Play continues until a clothespin is attached to each matching space on the board.

Bounce Game Board and Title

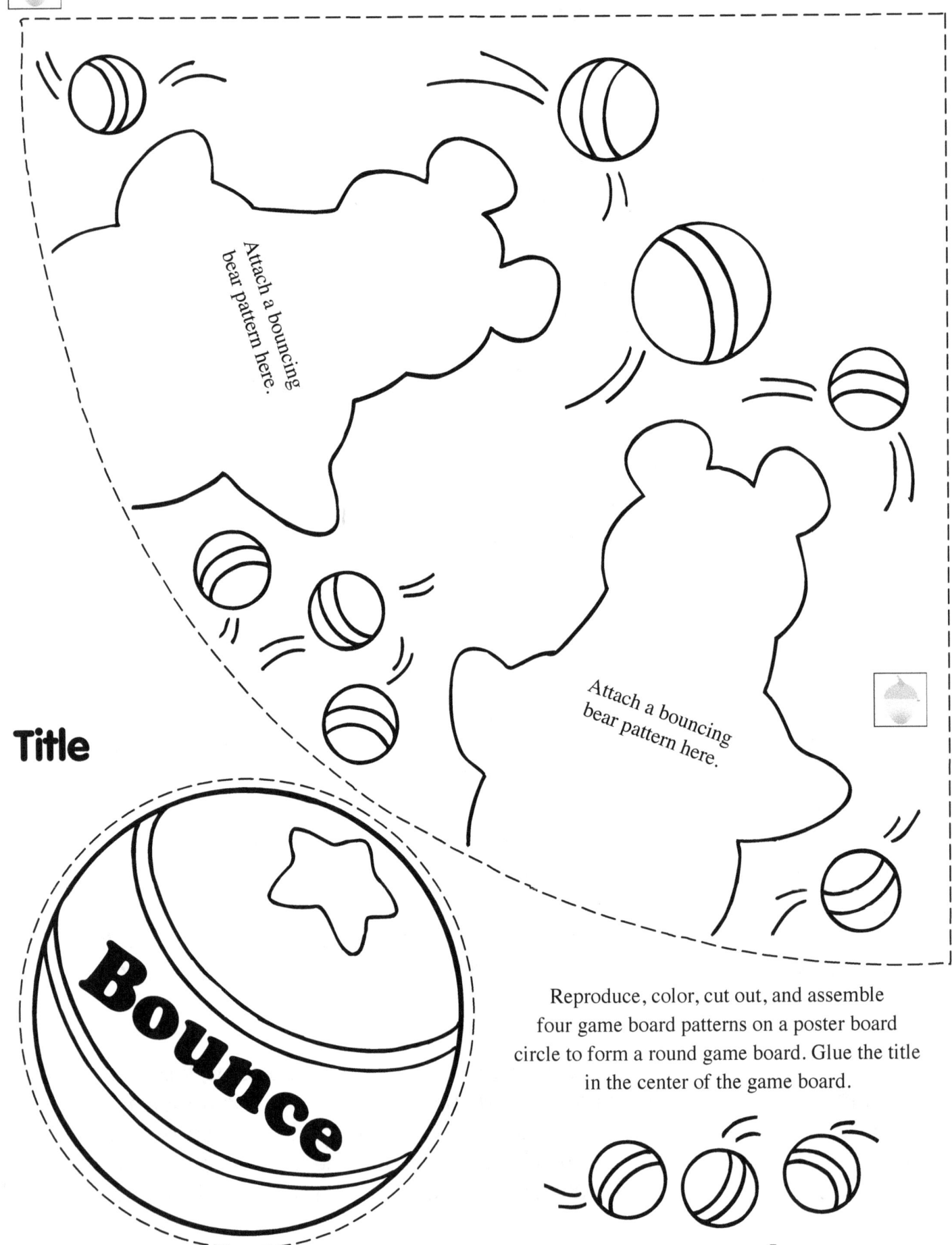

Reproduce, color, cut out, and assemble four game board patterns on a poster board circle to form a round game board. Glue the title in the center of the game board.

Bouncing Bear Patterns

Reproduce, color, cut out, and glue the bouncing bear patterns on the assembled game board.

Creative Option: Reproduce, color, and cut out a bouncing bear from poster board or oak tag. Measure, cut, and glue a gift wrap ball on the cutout. Glue a craft stick to the back of the bear to form a stick puppet.

Bouncing Bear Patterns

Reproduce, color, cut out, and glue the bouncing bear patterns on the assembled game board.

Creative Option: Reproduce, color, and cut out a bouncing bear from poster board or oak tag. Measure, cut, wrap, and tape an oak tag headband. Glue the bouncing bear cutout to the headband.

Bouncing Bear Patterns

Reproduce, color, cut out, and glue the bouncing bear patterns on the assembled game board.

Creative Option: Reproduce, color, and cut out the heart bouncing bear. Fold a sheet of colored construction paper in half to form a card. Glue the cutout on the front of the card. Write a message inside the card.

Bouncing Bear Patterns

Reproduce, color, cut out, and glue the bouncing bear patterns on the assembled game board.

Creative Option: Reproduce, color, and cut out the bouncing bears. Tape each cutout to a garland length of yarn. Hang the garland along the top of a door frame, along a window sill, or on a display board.

Ball Game Cards

Reproduce, color, and cut out a set of game cards for a game of Bounce.

Ships Ahoy!
A Clothespin Game
For Two Players

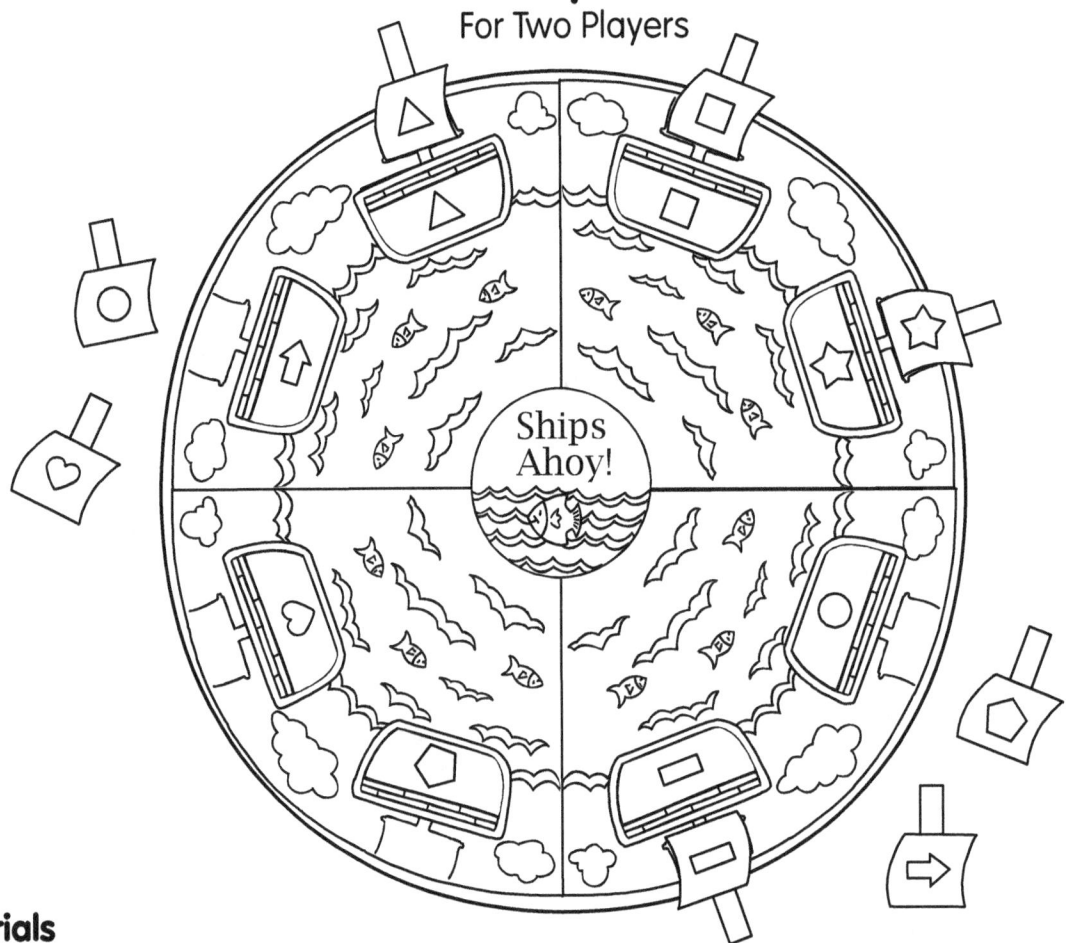

Materials
crayons, markers, scissors, glue, file folders, clothespins, large envelope

Assembly
Game Board: Reproduce, color, and cut out four game board patterns. Matching along the straight edges, glue the game board patterns on a poster board circle to form a round game board. Glue the title in the center of the game board. Then reproduce, color, cut out, and glue one set of ship patterns on the assembled game board. Note: Make multiple game boards to practice color, shape, and pattern recognition.

Clothespin Game Cards: Reproduce, color, and cut out a set of sail game cards to match the ship patterns on the assembled game board. Glue a clothespin to the back of each game card. Decorate a large envelope with drawings of ships and sea creatures. Store the clothespin game cards in the envelope. (Include non-matching game cards for advanced players, or all matches for early learners.)

How to Play
Set up the game board on a table. Place the clothespin game cards, face down, on the table. Each player, in turn, draws a clothespin. If there is a match, the player identifies the match, and clips the clothespin to the correct space. If there is no match, the player places the clothespin back on the table, face down. Play continues until a clothespin is attached to each matching space on the game board.

Ships Ahoy! Game Board and Title

Attach a ship here.

Attach a ship here.

Ships Ahoy!

Reproduce, color, cut out, and assemble four game board patterns on a poster board circle to form a round game board. Glue the title in the center of the game board.

Ship Patterns

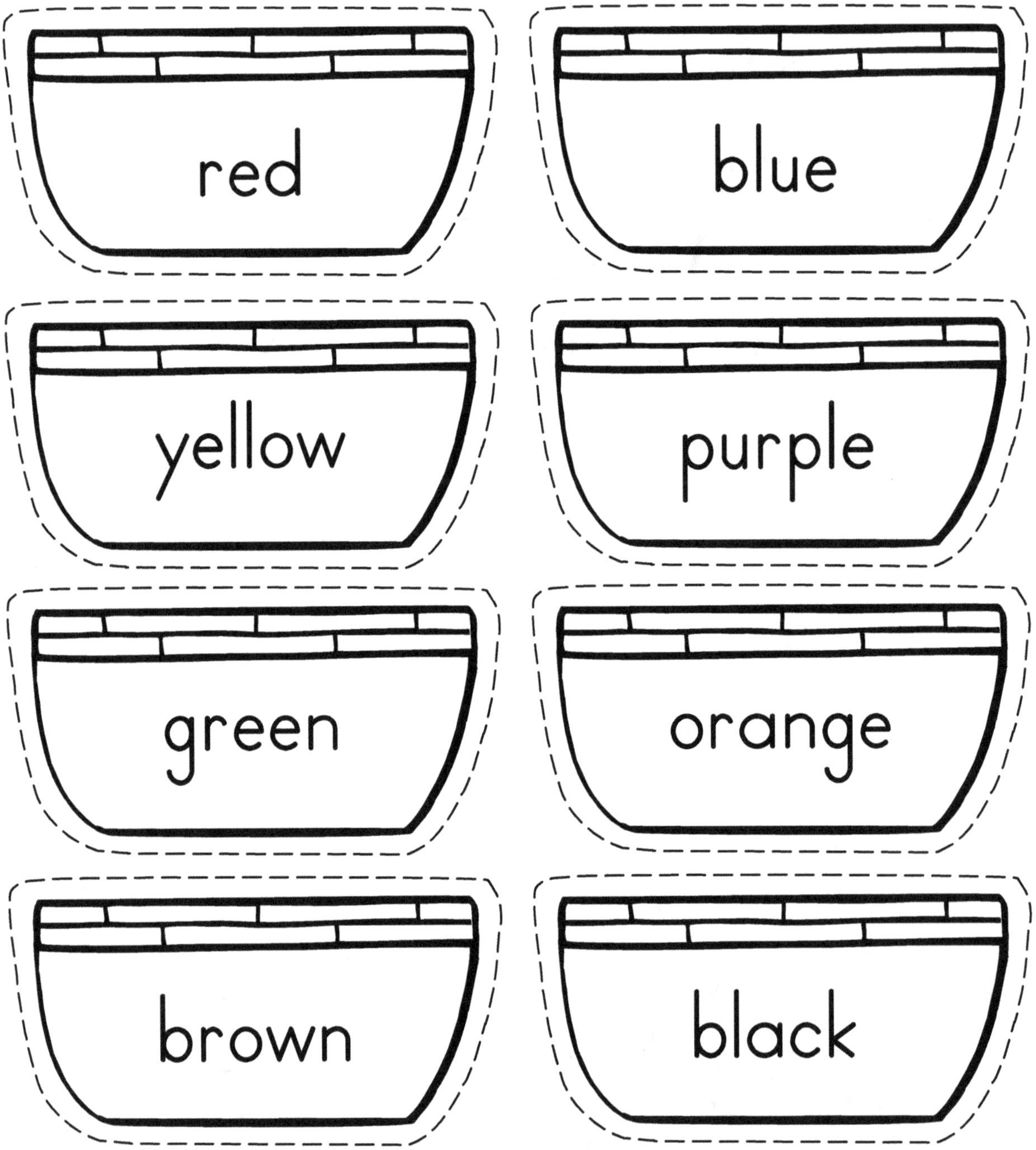

red

blue

yellow

purple

green

orange

brown

black

Reproduce, color, cut out, and glue one set of ship patterns on an assembled Ships Ahoy! game board. Use with sail game cards on page 35.

Ship Patterns

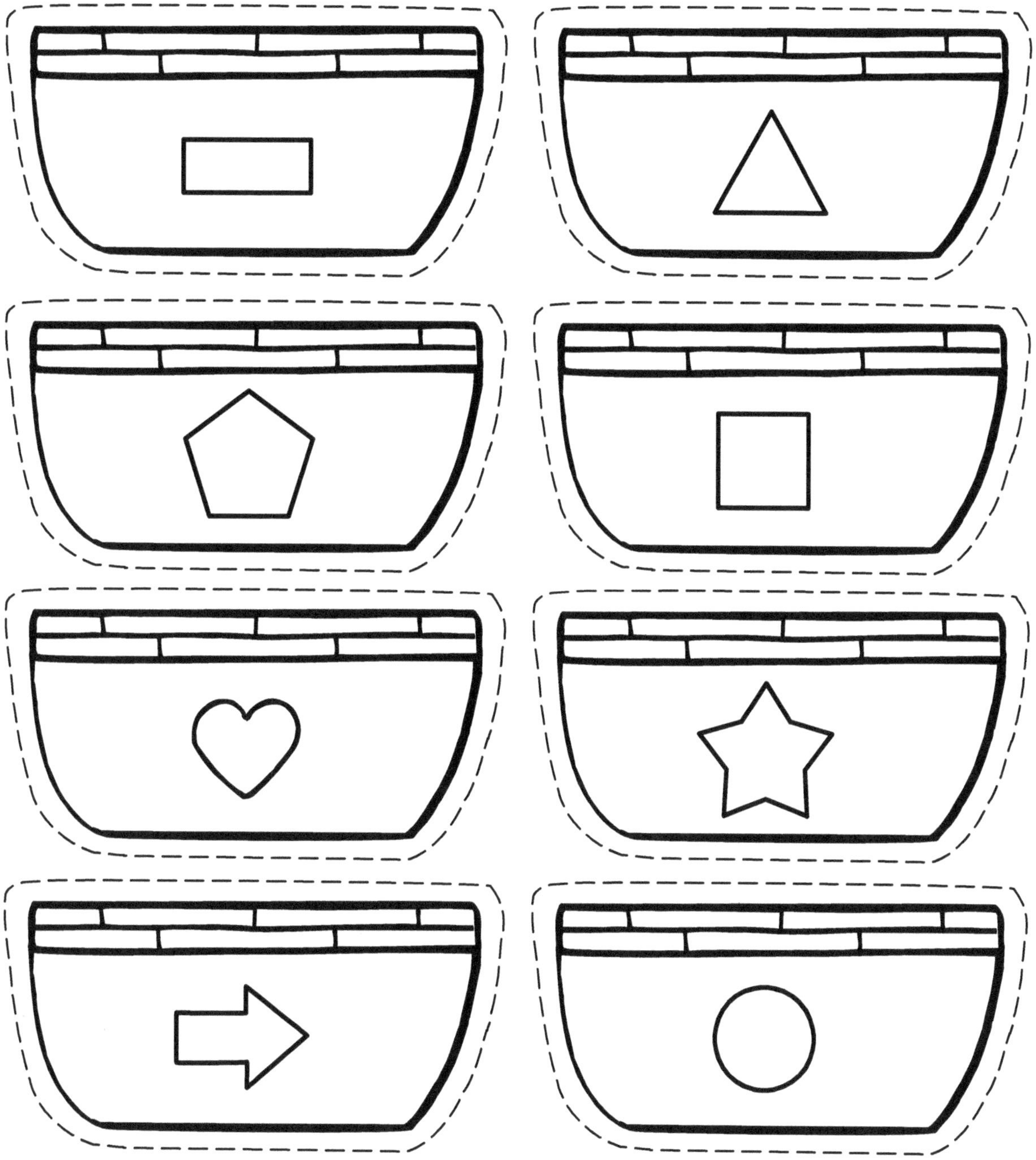

Reproduce, color, cut out, and glue one set of ship patterns on an assembled Ships Ahoy! game board.

Creative Option: Color and cut out sail and matching ship patterns.
Glue small crafts sticks between matching ships and sails on a sheet of construction paper.
Draw waves, clouds, and sea creatures to complete the pictures.

Ship Patterns

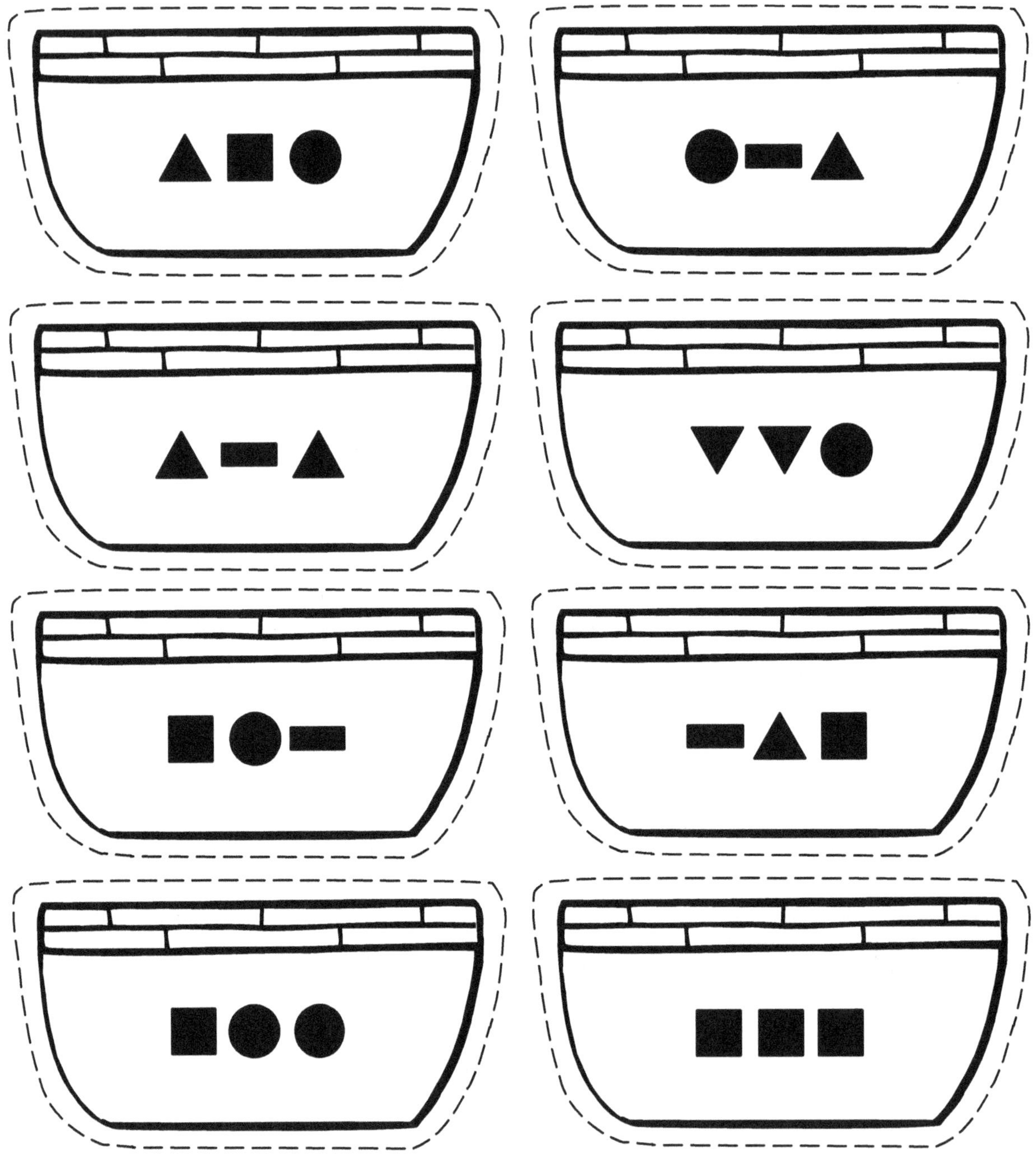

Reproduce, color, cut out, and glue one set of ship patterns on an assembled Ships Ahoy! game board.

Sail Game Cards

Reproduce, color, and cut out one set of game cards for a game of Ships Ahoy!
Use with boat patterns on page 32.

Color the sail game cards as follows:

apple=red	corn=yellow	blueberries=blue
carrots=orange	beans=green	grapes=purple
pretzel=brown	licorice=black	

Sail Game Cards

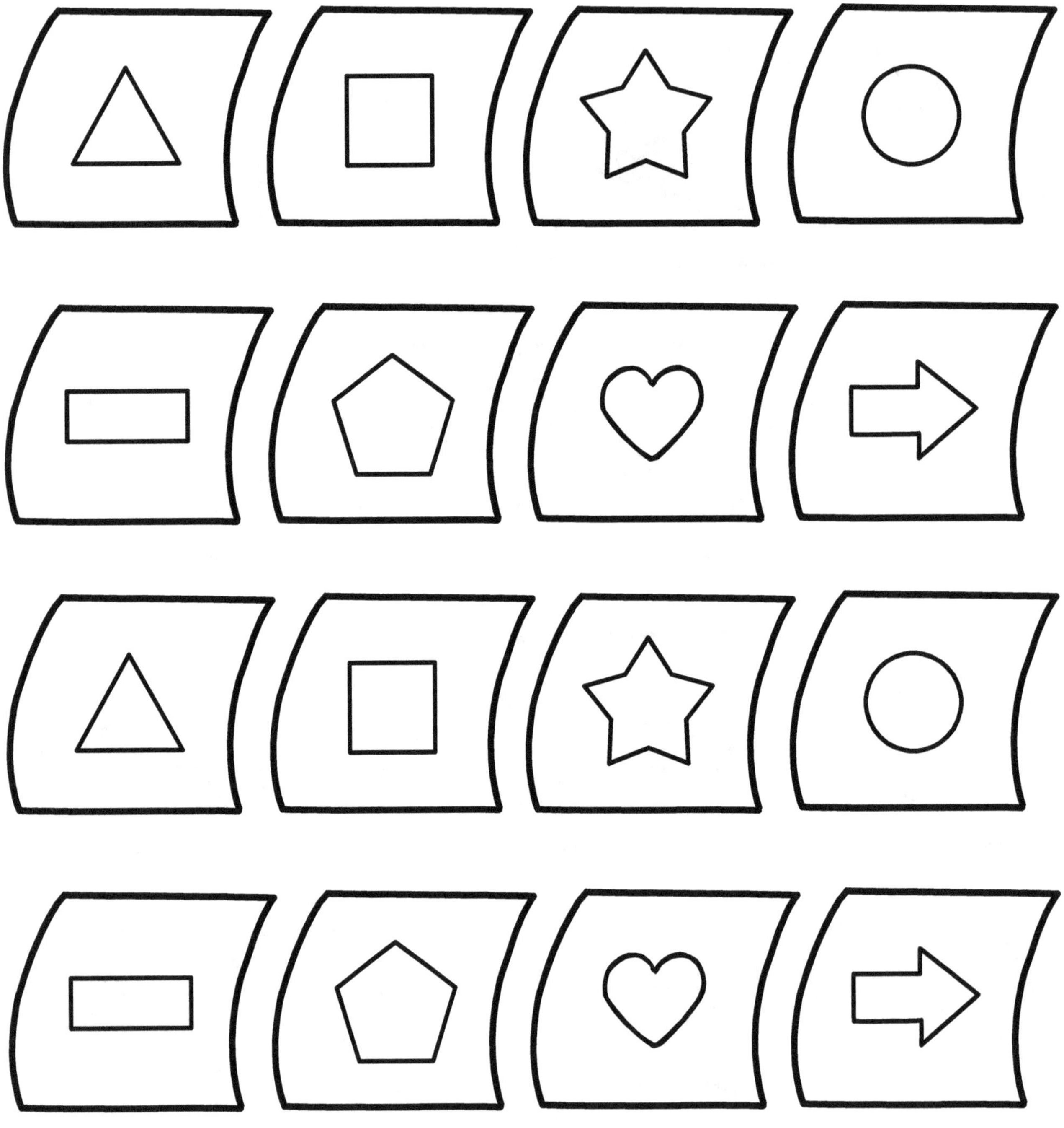

Reproduce, color, and cut out one set of game cards for a game of Ships Ahoy!

Sail Game Cards

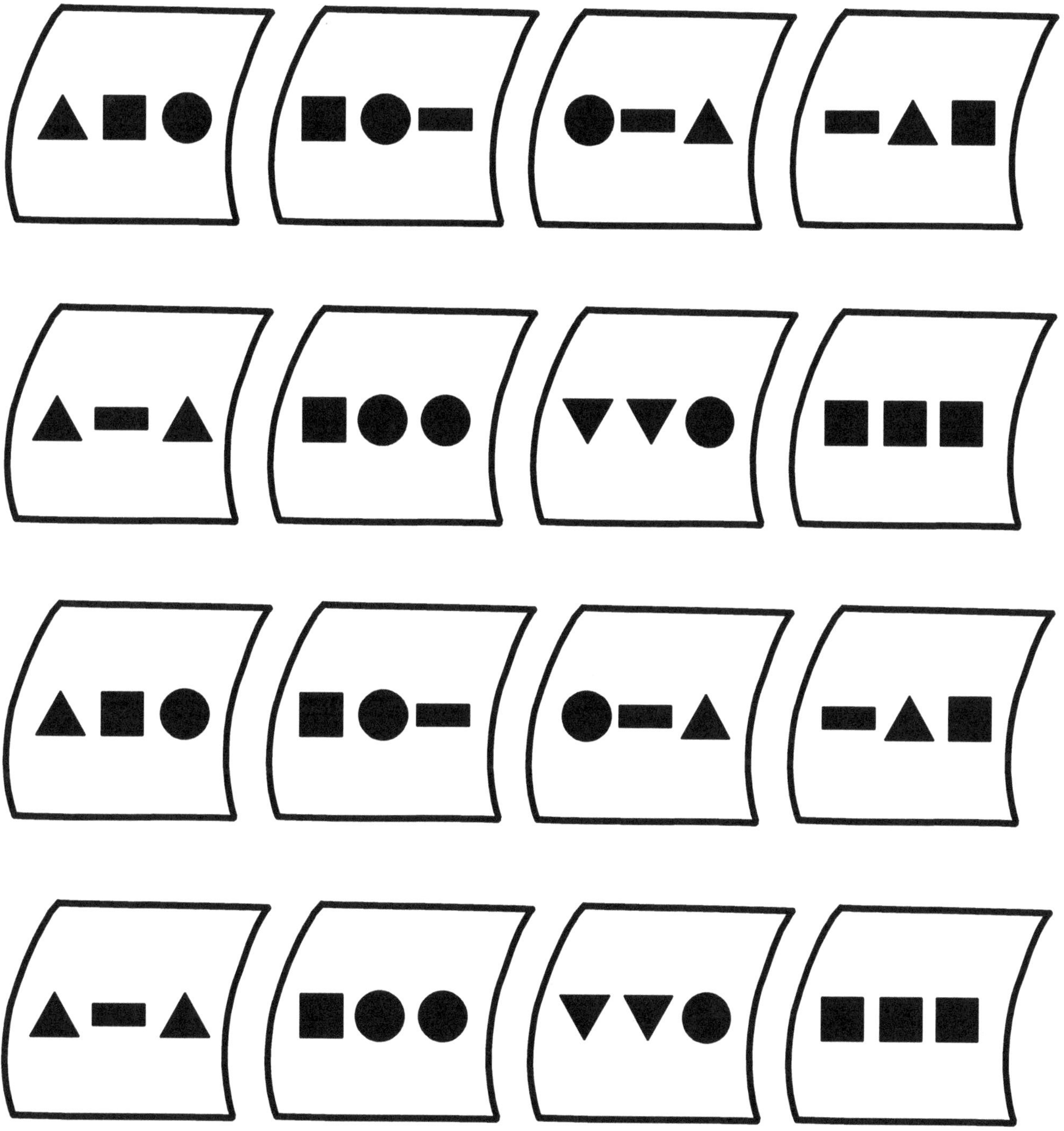

Reproduce, color, and cut out one set of game cards for a game of Ships Ahoy!

Paint a Palette
A Clothespin Game
For Two Players

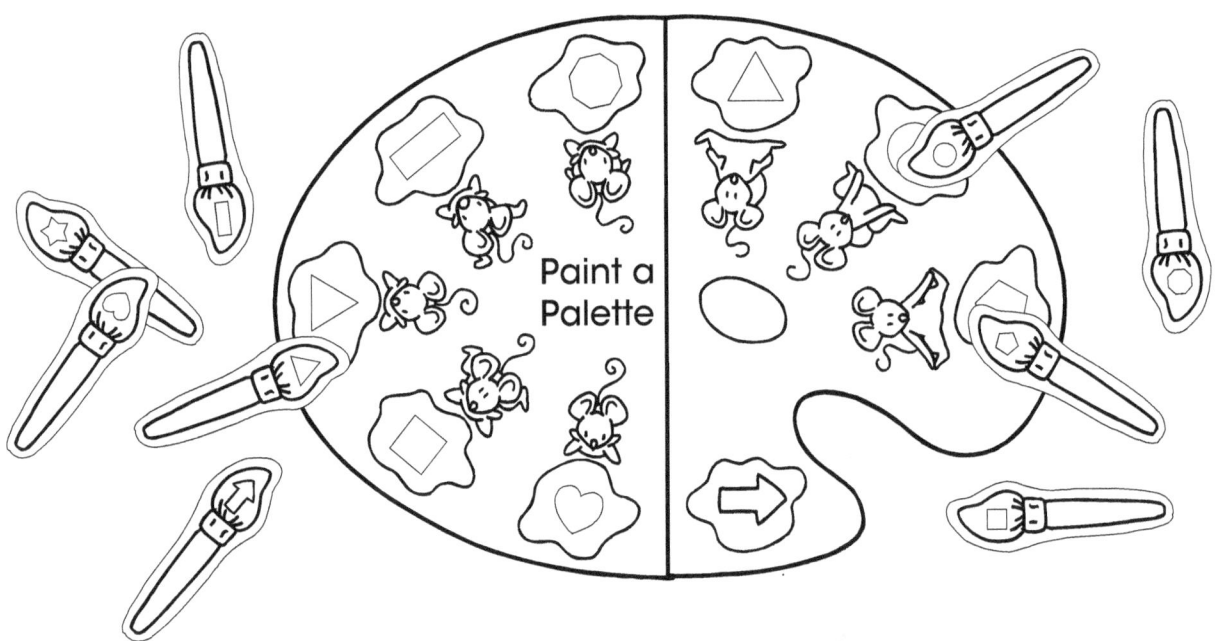

Materials
crayons, markers, scissors, glue, file folders, clothespins, large envelope

Assembly
Game Board: Reproduce, color, and cut out the game board patterns. Matching along the straight edges, glue the game board patterns on a poster board oval. Trim around the edges to form a paint palette game board.

Clothespin Game Cards: Reproduce, color, and cut out a set of paintbrush game cards. Color the blank paintbrushes to match the paint spots on the game board. Glue a clothespin to the back of each game card. Decorate a large envelope with different color paintbrush cutouts. Store the clothespin game cards in the envelope. (Include non-matching game cards for advanced players, or all matches for early learners.)

How to Play
Set up the game board on a table. Place the clothespin game cards, face down, on the table. Each player, in turn, draws a clothespin. If there is a match, the player identifies the match, and clips the clothespin to the correct space. If there is no match, the player places the clothespin back on the table, face down. Play continues until a clothespin is attached to each matching space on the game board.

Paint a Palette Game Board

Reproduce, color, and cut out the game board patterns. Matching along the straight edges, glue the game board patterns on a poster board oval. Trim around the edges to form a paint palette game board.

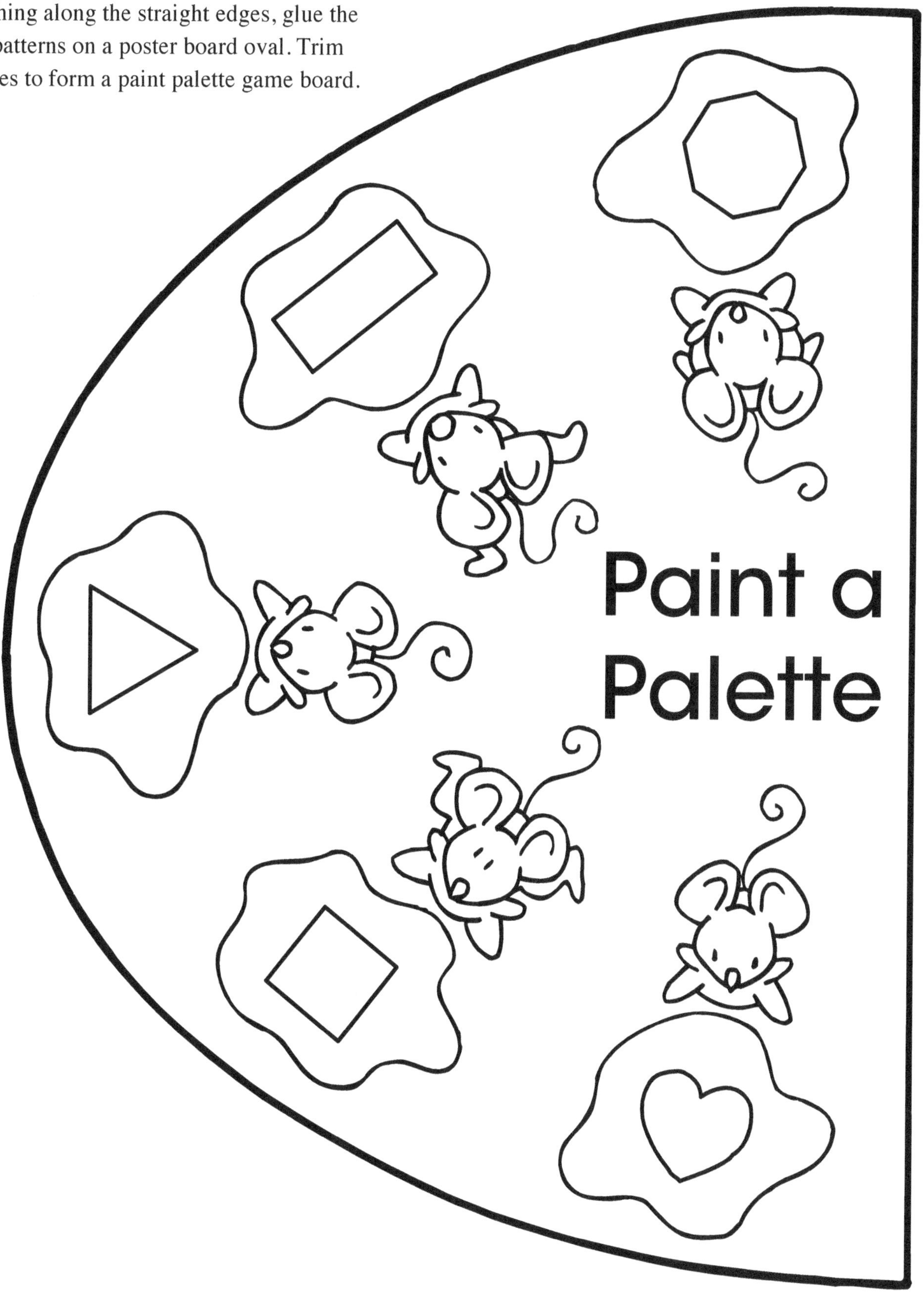

Paint a Palette

Paint a Palette Game Board

Reproduce, color, and cut out the game board patterns. Matching along the straight edges, glue the game board patterns on a poster board oval. Trim around the edges to form a paint palette game board.

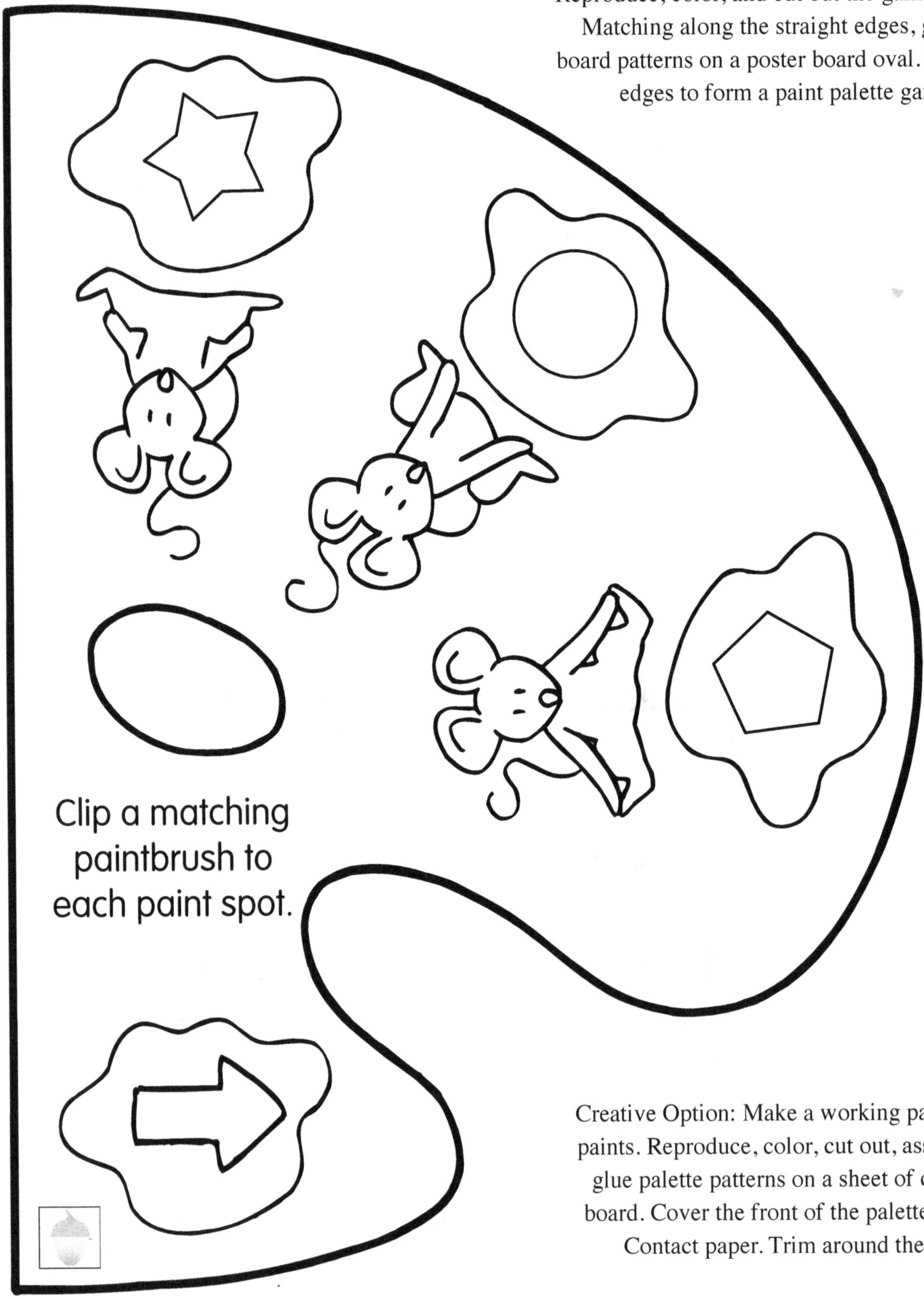

Clip a matching paintbrush to each paint spot.

Creative Option: Make a working palette to mix paints. Reproduce, color, cut out, assemble, and glue palette patterns on a sheet of corrugated board. Cover the front of the palette with clear Contact paper. Trim around the edges.

Paintbrush Game Cards

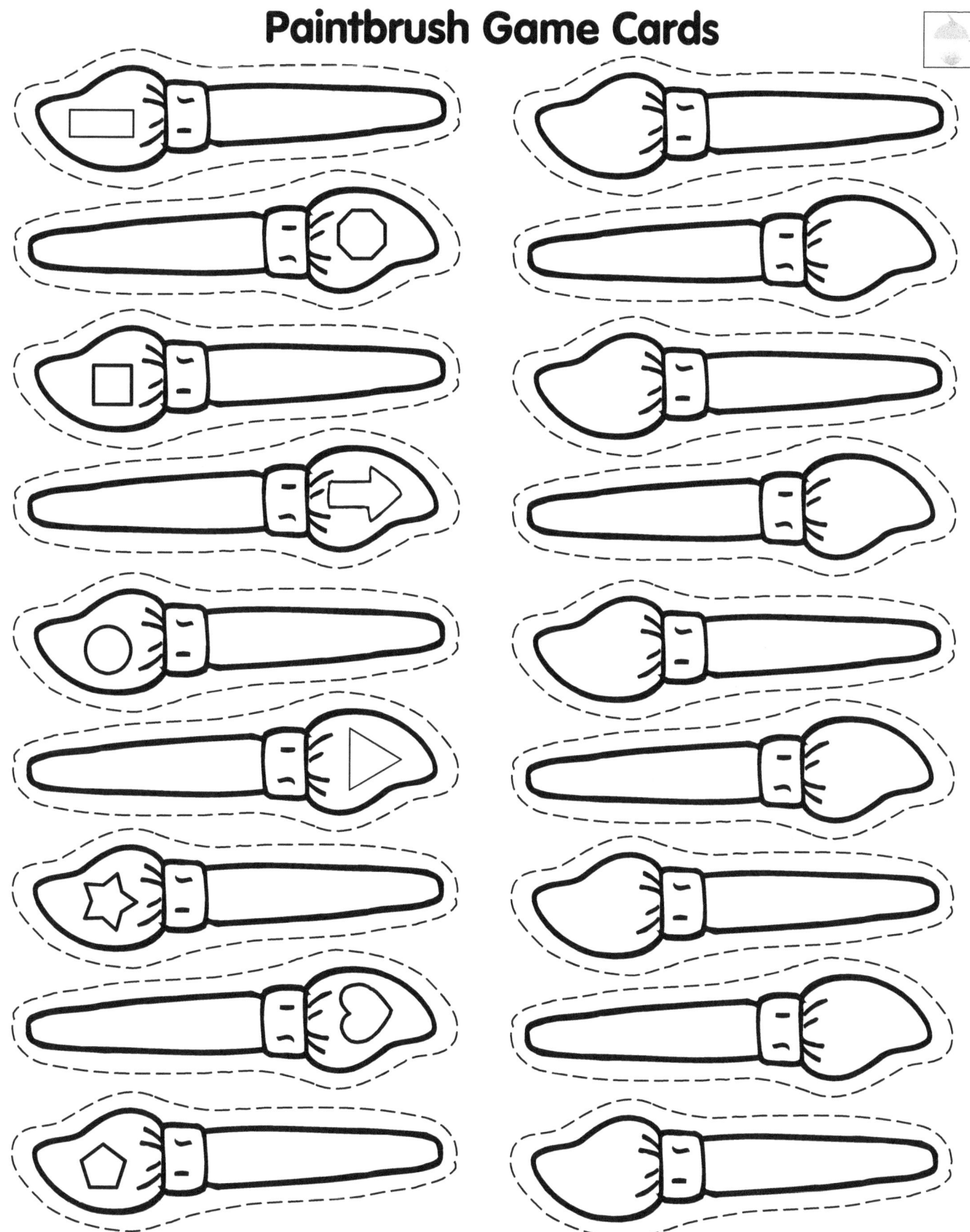

Reproduce, color, and cut out the paintbrushes.
Option: Color the blank brushes red, blue, yellow, green, purple, orange, black, brown, and gray for a color matching activity. Glue a clothespin to the back of each paintbrush. Program the palette with matching colors.

Knock Knock
A Match Board Game
For Two Players

Materials
crayons, markers, scissors, glue, file folder, envelope

Assembly
Game Board: Reproduce, color, and cut out the cover and game board patterns. Glue each game board pattern to the inside of a folder. Glue the cover to the front of the folder, then laminate. Tape an envelope to the back of the game board folder to store game cards.

Game Cards: Reproduce, color, laminate, then cut out the game cards. Option: Reproduce, color, and glue the game cards page to the back of a sheet of gift wrap, then laminate and cut out the cards. Store the game cards in the envelope on the back of the game board folder.

How to Play
Set up the game board on a table. Each player chooses a side of the board to play. One player shuffles and places the key game cards, face down, on the table. Each player, in turn, draws a card. If there is a match, the player identifies the match, and places the key card on the correct door. If there is no match, the player places the card, face down, in a discard pile. Play continues until each player has placed a matching key on every door on his or her game board.

Knock Knock Cover

Knock Knock

Knock Knock Game Board

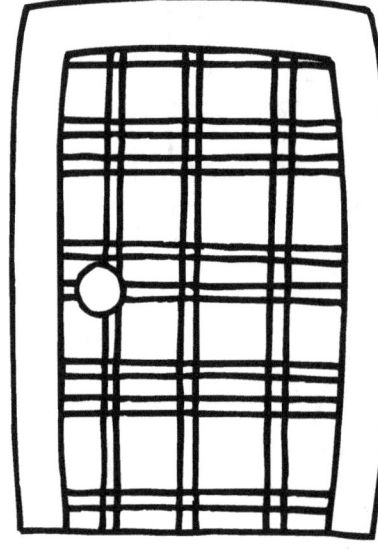
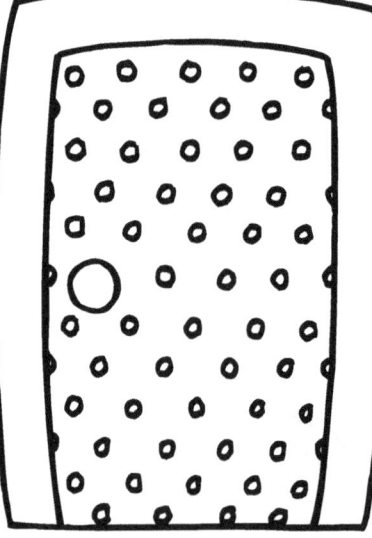
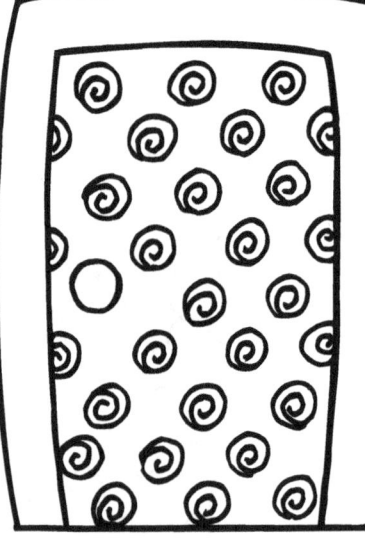
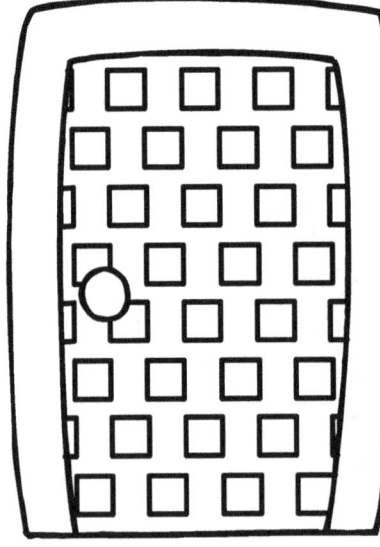

Knock Knock Game Board

Place a matching key on each door.

Key Game Cards

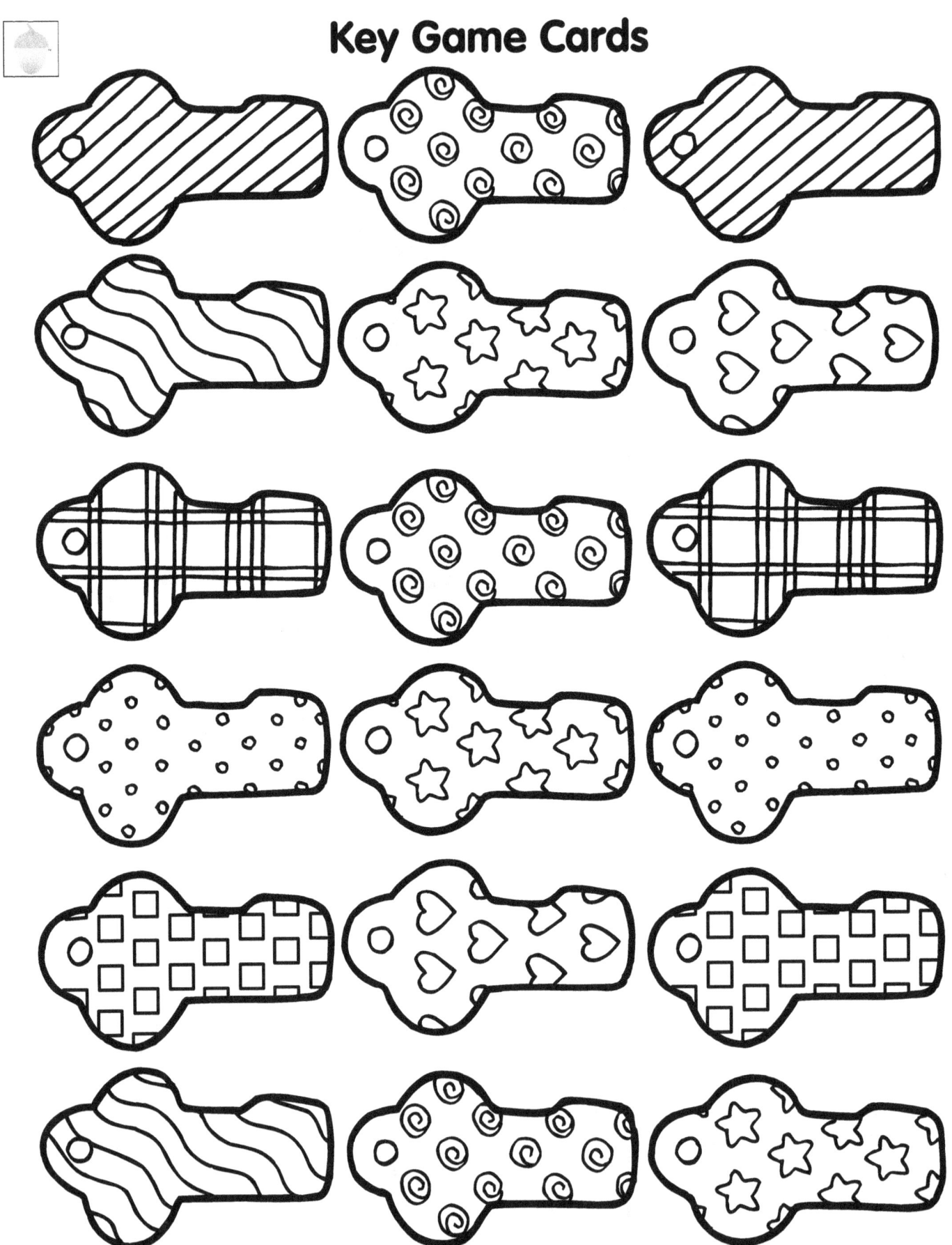

Reproduce, color, and cut out the game cards for a game of Knock Knock.

Creative Option: Copy keys onto heavy paper. Laminate and cut out.
Punch a hole in each key. Lace the keys on a yarn key ring.

Door Patterns and Key Game Cards

Reproduce and decorate additional matching pattern, color, or shape doors and keys for more matching skills practice.

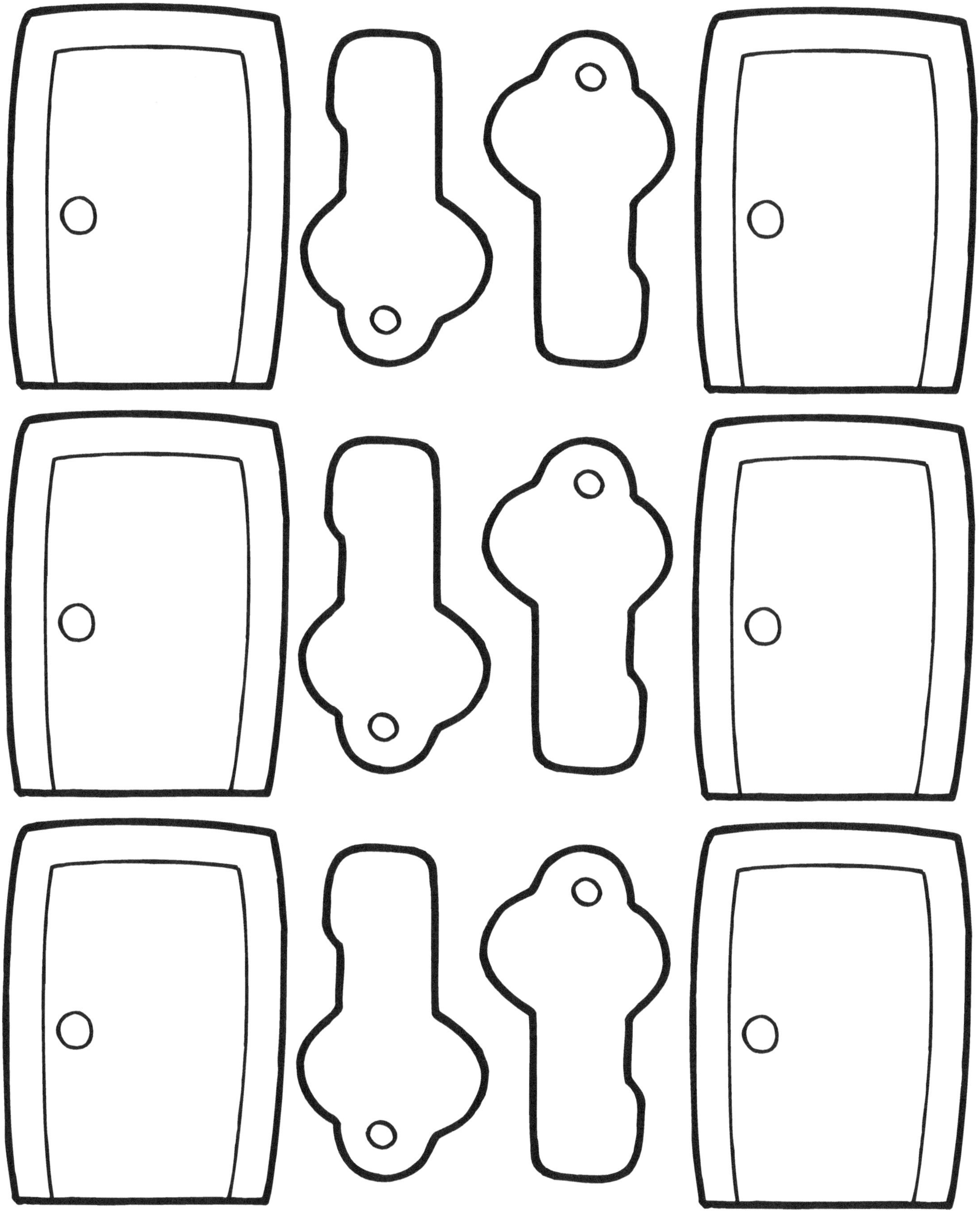

Turnip Patch Match
A Match Board Game
For Two Players

Materials
crayons, markers, scissors, glue, file folder, envelope, basket

Assembly
Game Board: Reproduce, color, and cut out the cover and game board patterns. Glue each game board pattern to the inside of a folder. Glue the cover to the front of the folder, then laminate. Tape an envelope to the back of the game board folder to store game cards. See page 52 for alternate programming options.

Game Cards: Reproduce, color, laminate, then cut out two sets of game cards. Option: Reproduce, color, and glue each page of game cards to the back of a sheet of gift wrap, then laminate and cut out the cards. Store the game cards in the envelope on the back of the game board folder. Note: Make multiple game boards to practice color, shape, and pattern recognition.

How to Play
Set up the game board on a table. Each player chooses a side of the board to play. One player shuffles and places the turnip game cards, face down, in a basket. Each player, in turn, draws a card. If there is a match, the player identifies the match, and places the card on the correct groundhog. If there is no match, the player places the card, face down, in a discard pile. Play continues until each player has placed a matching turnip on every groundhog on his or her game board.

Turnip Patch Match Cover

Turnip Patch Match

Turnip Patch Match Game Board

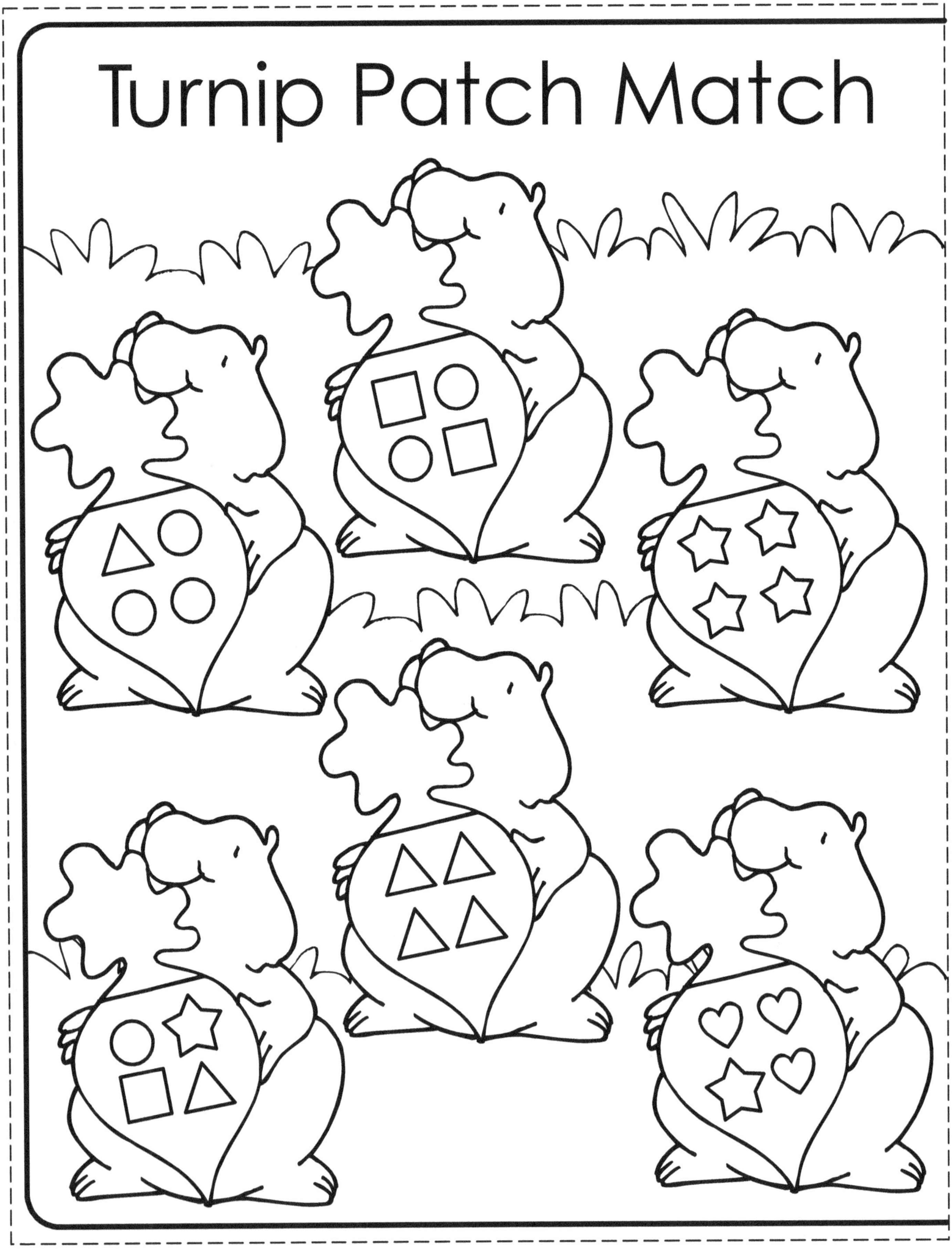

Turnip Patch Match

Turnip Patch Match Game Board

Match the turnips.

Turnip Game Cards

Reproduce, color, and cut out one set of game cards for a game of Turnip Patch Match.

Programming Options:
- Program the turnips on the game boards with twelve different color word turnips (p. 53). Then reproduce a set of matching color construction paper turnip game cards to match the color word turnips on each game board.
- Program the turnips on the game boards with twelve different shape turnips (p. 53). Then reproduce a set of shape turnip game cards to match the shape turnips on each game board.

Turnip Game Cards

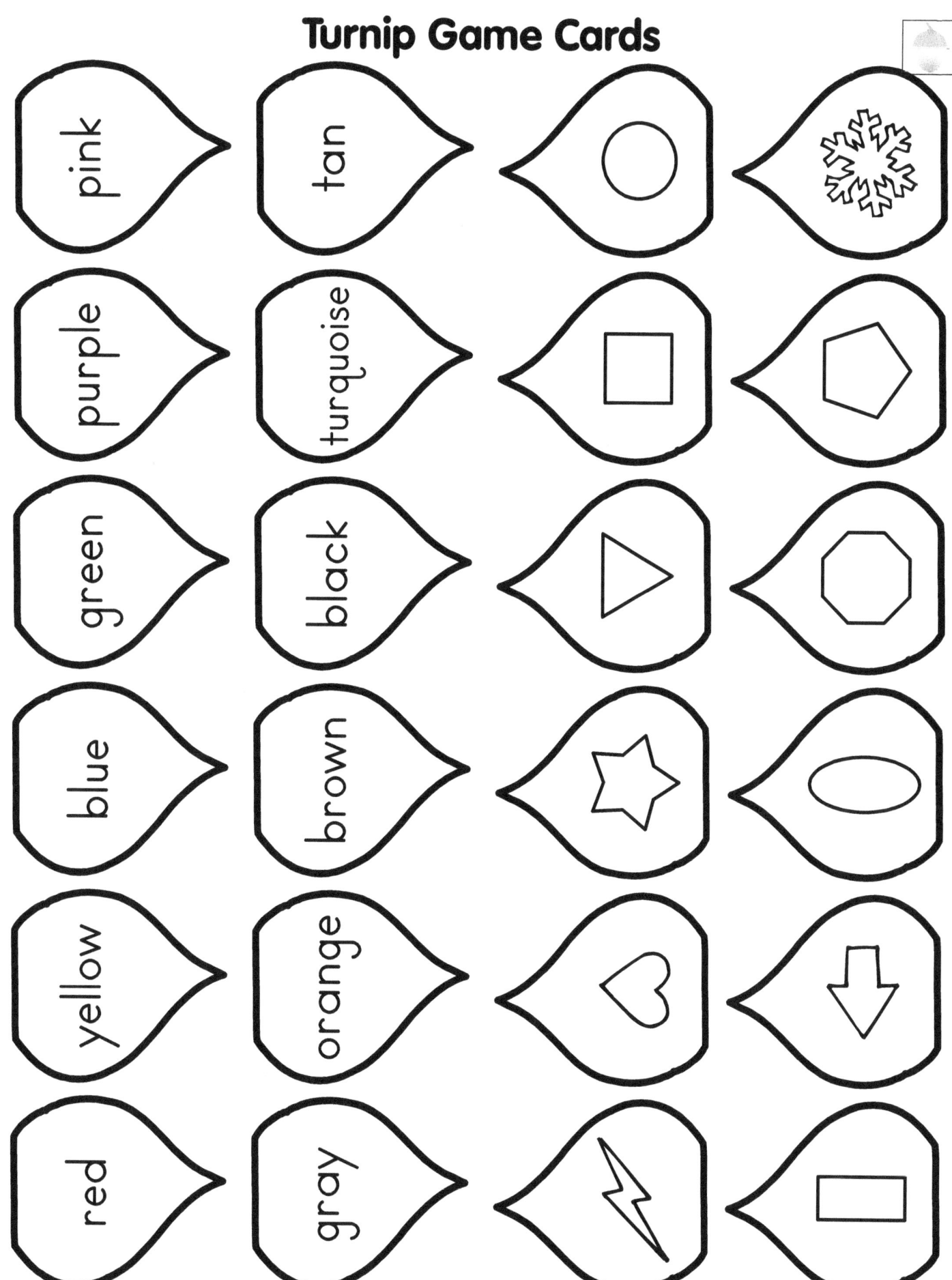

Reproduce, color, and cut out one set of color word or shape game cards for a game of Turnip Patch Match.

Duck, Duck, Goose
A Match Board Game
For Two Players

Materials
crayons, markers, scissors, glue, file folder, envelope, paper bag

Assembly
Game Board: Reproduce, color, and cut out the cover and game board patterns. Glue each game board pattern to the inside of a folder. Glue the cover to the front of the folder, then laminate. Tape an envelope to the back of the game board folder to store game cards.

Game Cards: Reproduce, color, laminate, then cut out two sets of game cards. Option: Reproduce, color, and glue each page of game cards to the back of a sheet of gift wrap, then laminate and cut out the cards. Store the game cards in the envelope on the back of the game board folder.

How to Play
Set up the game board on a table. Place the cards in a paper bag. Each player, in turn, draws a card. If there is a match, the player identifies the match, and places the card on the correct duck or goose. If there is no match, the player places the card, face down, in a discard pile. Play continues until each player has placed a card on each matching space on the match board. Place the discarded cards back in the bag if needed.

Duck, Duck, Goose Cover

Duck, Duck, Goose

Duck, Duck, Goose Game Board

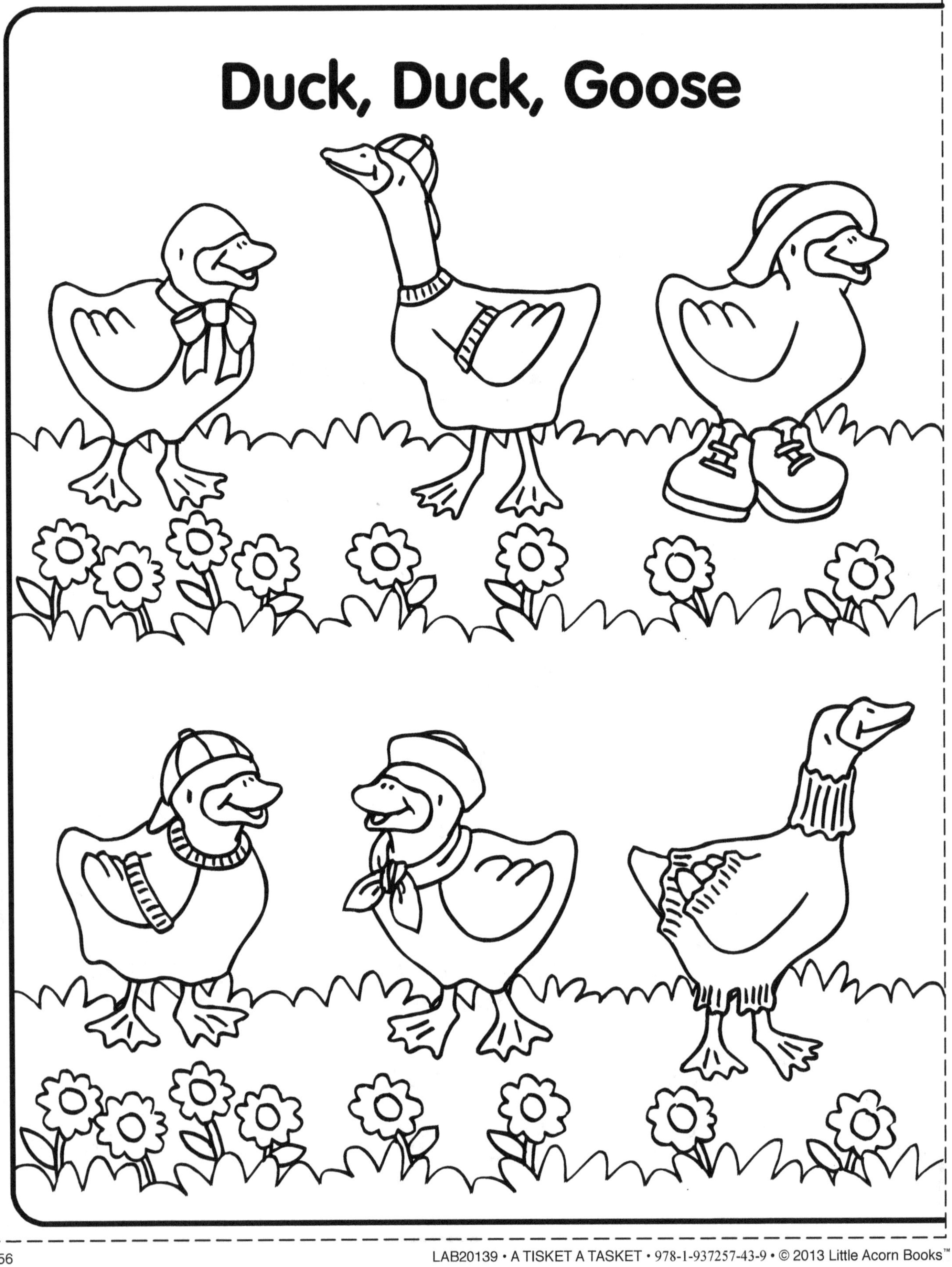

Duck, Duck, Goose

Duck, Duck, Goose Game Board

Place a matching game card on each duck and goose.

Goose Game Cards

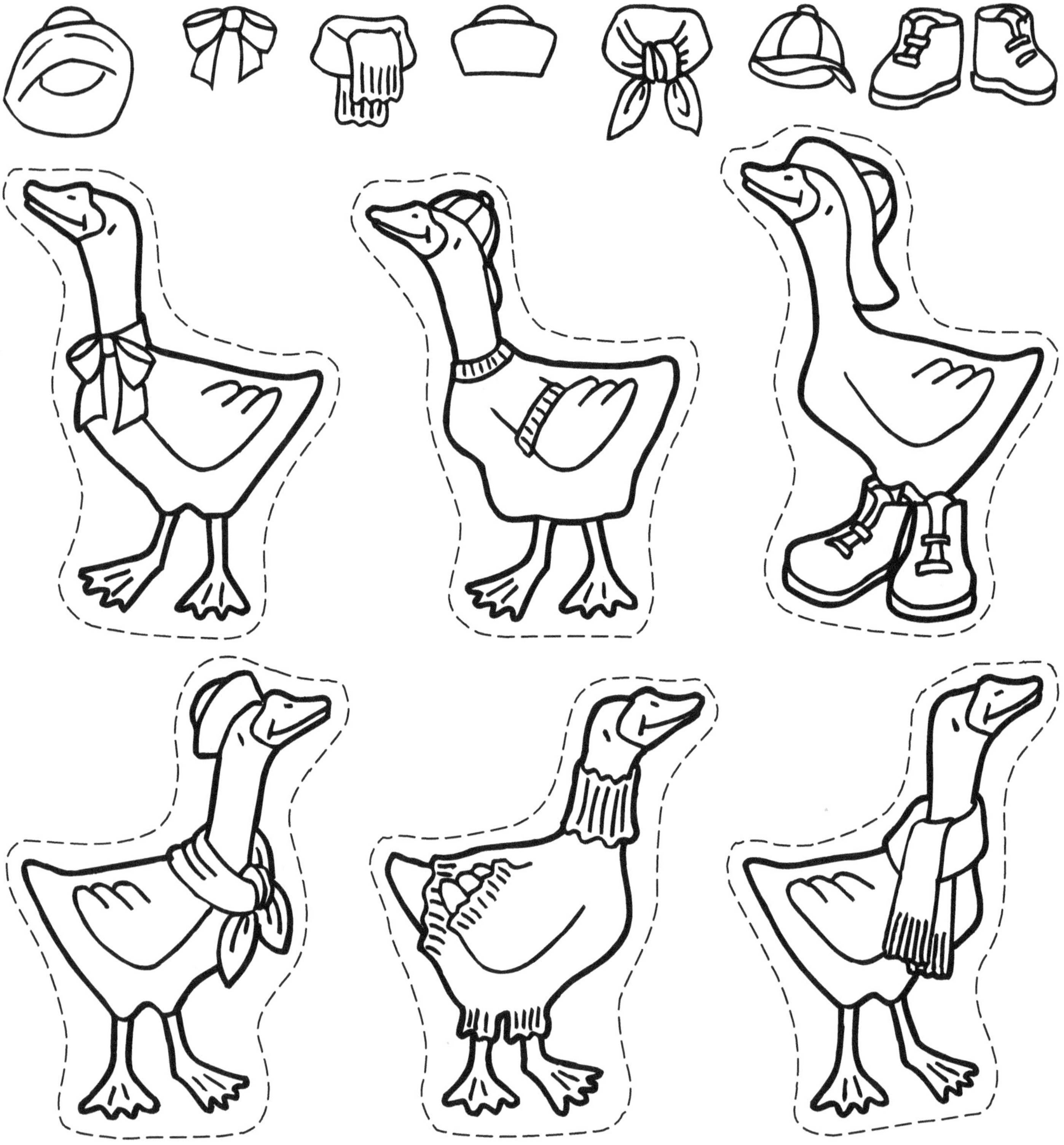

Reproduce, color, and cut out two sets of cards.

Creative Option: Reproduce, color, cut out, arrange, then glue the goose cards on a sheet of construction paper. Decorate the construction paper. Glue a yarn border around the picture.

Duck Game Cards

Reproduce, color, and cut out two sets of cards.

Creative Option: Reproduce, color, cut out, and glue the ducks on a sheet of construction paper. Glue green yarn lengths for grass, cotton balls for clouds, and colored pom poms for flowers.

Hat Stackers
A Stacker Game
For One to Two Players

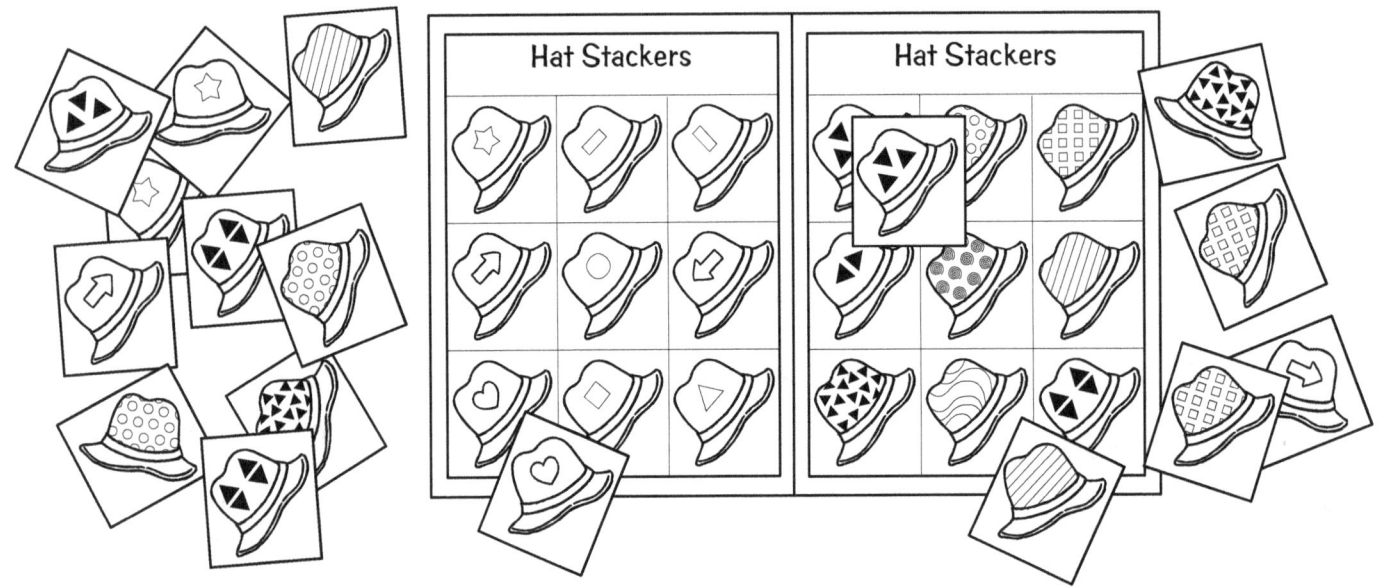

Materials

crayons, markers, scissors, glue, file folder, envelope

Assembly

Game Board: Reproduce, color, and cut out the hat stackers game board patterns. Glue each game board pattern to the inside of a folder. Decorate the front of the folder with photographs of hats cut from magazines or game card cutouts, then laminate. Tape an envelope to the back of the game board folder to store game cards.

Game Cards: Reproduce, color, laminate, then cut apart two sets of game cards. Option: Reproduce, color, and glue each page of game cards to the back of a sheet of gift wrap, then laminate and cut apart the cards. Store the game cards in the envelope on the back of the game board folder.

How to Play

Set up the stacker game and cards on a table. One player shuffles and places the card deck, face down, on the table. Each player, in turn, draws, and stacks the drawn card on the matching space on the game board. Play continues until all the cards have been played.

Option: Use the game cards to play a game of Concentration. Shuffle and place all the cards, face down, on a table. Each player, in turn, turns over any two cards to find a match. If the player finds a match, he or she takes the cards and the next player takes a turn. If there is no match, each card is turned back over in the same position. Play continues until all the cards are taken.

Hat Stackers Game Board

Hat Stackers
Stack the matching shape hats.

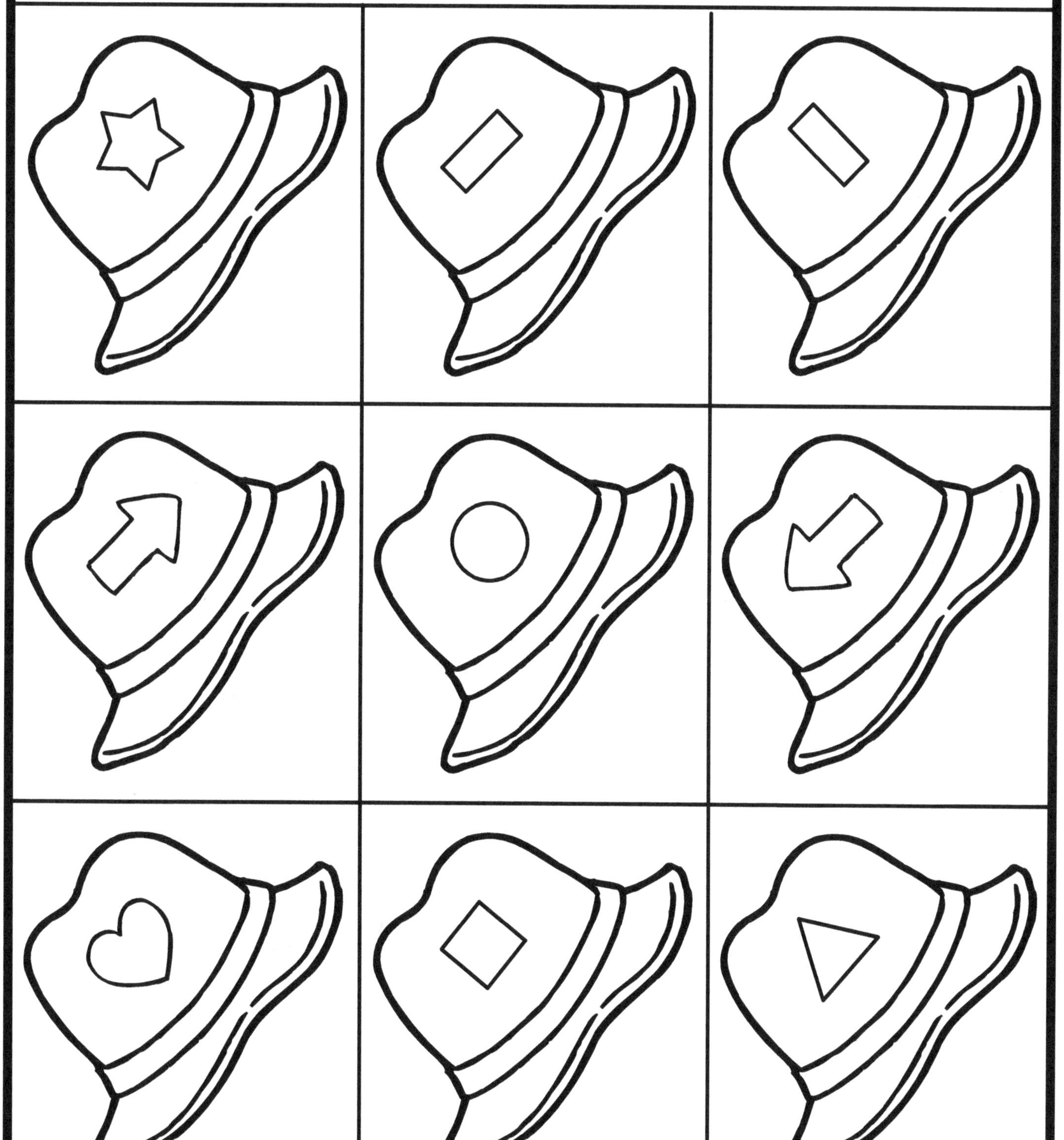

Hat Stackers Game Board

Hat Stackers
Stack the matching pattern hats.

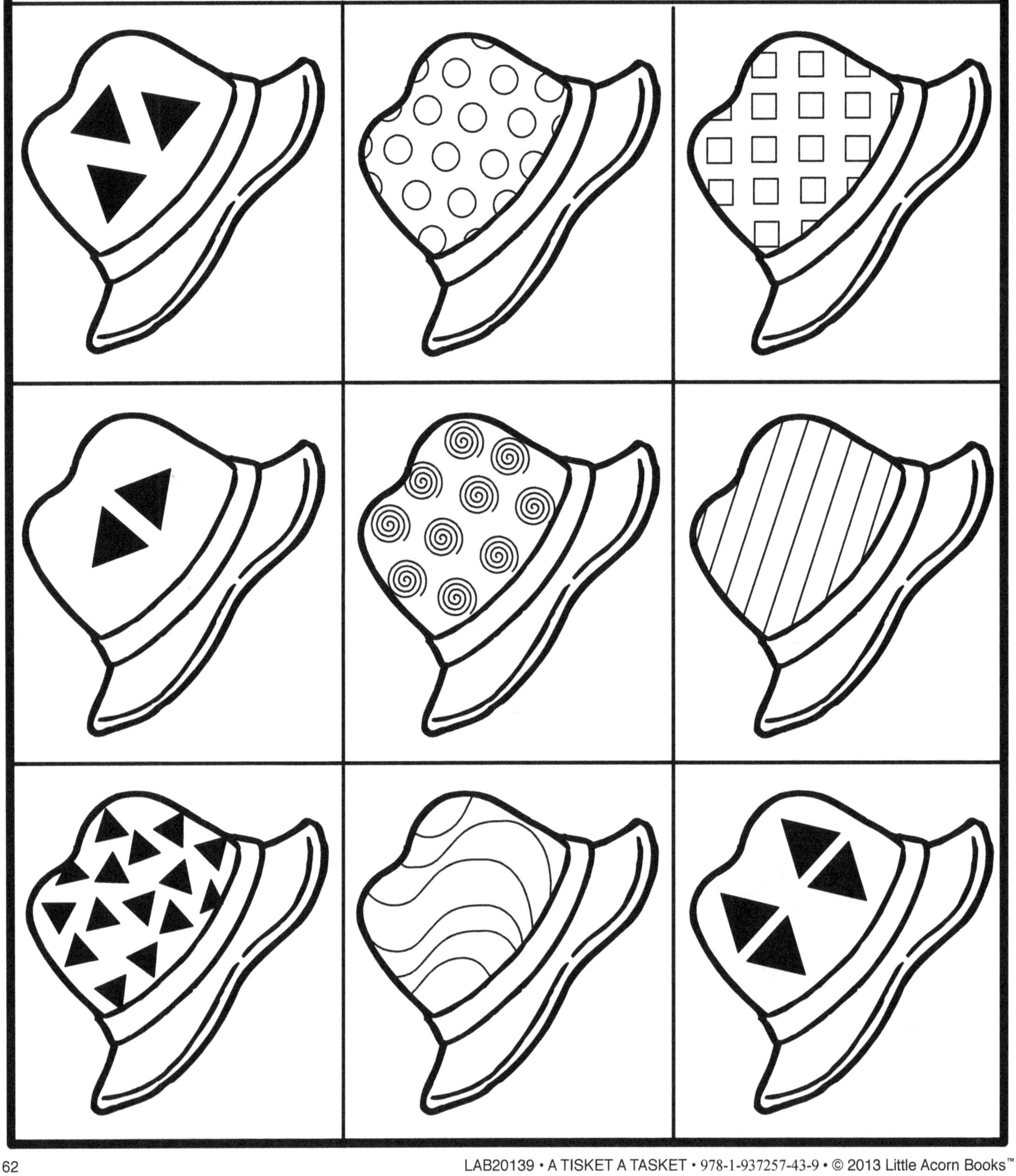

Hat Game Cards

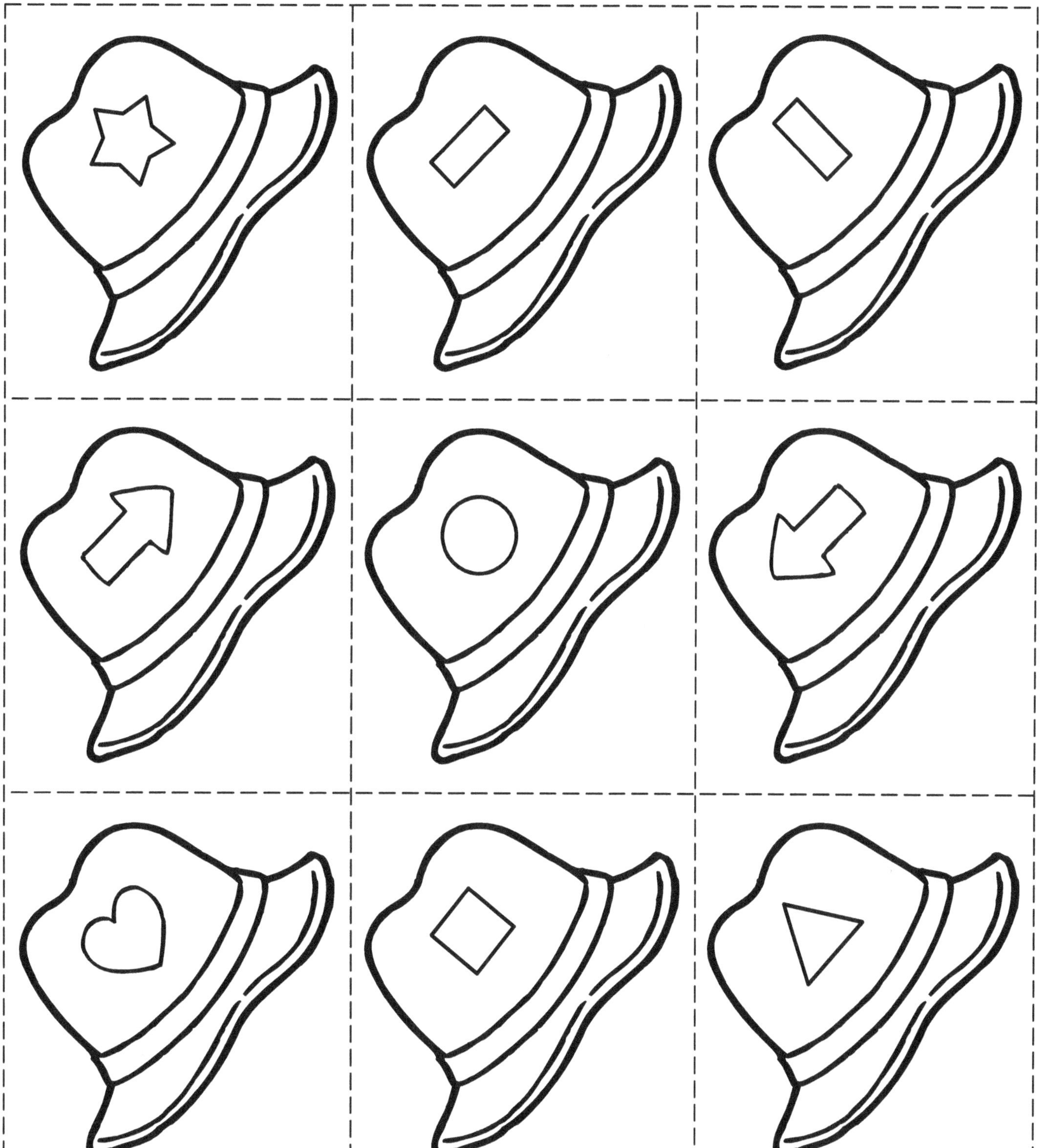

Reproduce, color, and cut apart two sets of game cards.

Hat Game Cards

Reproduce, color, and cut apart two sets of game cards.

64   LAB20139 • A TISKET A TASKET • 978-1-937257-43-9 • © 2013 Little Acorn Books™

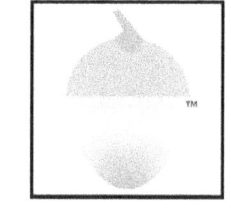

Little Acorn Books™

Promoting Early Skills for a Lifetime™

A Hands-on Picture Book Series • Infancy–Age 4

Miss Pitty Pat & Friends
Preschool–Grade 1

Mookie's Christmas Tree
For All Ages and Not Just for Christmas

Using Crayons, Scissors, & Glue for Crafts
Preschool–Grade 1

Little Acorn Books™
Visit our web site:
www.littleacornbooks.com

LAB20139 • A TISKET A TASKET • 978-1-937257-43-9 • © 2014 Little Acorn Books™

www.ingramcontent.com/pod-product-compliance
Lightning Source LLC
Chambersburg PA
CBHW081020040426
42444CB00014B/3286